GUY BLEWS was born [illegible] England.
He currently lives in Malibu, California.

To my Mum, for always allowing me to question,
to comment and to make my own decisions.
Thank you for this, and for so much more.

In loving memory of my Sweet, Sweet Angel – I miss you always, more than I can ever explain. I try to fill my tears with joy. Love. Love. Love.

Special thanks to Simon Hammerson for giving me the encouragement to write this book.

To Justin Marciano for believing that people would read it.

To Nick Taussig for his dedication with the edit, and to the cause.

Marriage & How to Avoid it

A truly cynical guide

GUY BLEWS

REVOLVER BOOKS
Published by Revolver Books © 2006 a division of Revolver Entertainment Ltd
PO Box 31643
London
W11 2XS
UK

Revolver Entertainment Ltd, Registered Offices: Craven House, 16 Northumberland Avenue, London WC2N 5AP

A CIP catalogue record for this book is available from the British Library

ISBN 10: 0-9549407-3-3
ISBN 13: 978-0-9549407-3-7

Cover design by RNR

Text design and typesetting by Dexter Haven Associates Ltd, London

Printed and bound in Great Britain by Bookmarque Ltd, Croydon

Contents

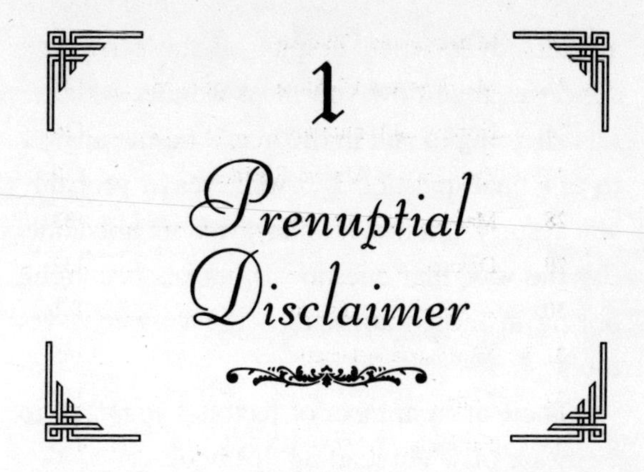

1 Prenuptial Disclaimer

This is a book that will, ultimately, offer you the truth. It will also offer you an opportunity, an alternative, a way out. I am not just being a know-it-all here: marriage *is* an utter waste of time, money and effort!

In this respect, this book is like a prenuptial. It is written to provide comfort and support for those people who have doubts about marriage. You are probably one of them, otherwise why would you be reading this now? And you have most likely asked the same questions that I will pose in the following pages: is it worth it? Is it necessary? Is it outdated? Is it just another item on the shopping list of life? Is it true that sex becomes boring in most marriages? And if you are already married despite all these nagging concerns, then now you must wonder whether it is all going to end in divorce. And the answer to this final question is…well, yes, it probably will… sorry. But hey, it's okay: you are not alone. (By the way, that question about sex becoming boring in most marriages – the answer is yes too!)

There are a number of factors I want you to be aware of when reading this book.

Firstly, it is imperative you read it with a light-hearted inflection. Although some of the points raised are intended to be perfectly serious, they are written in a playful, and I must confess slightly provocative tone, and should be read thus.

Secondly, I am assuming that you, the reader, are a relatively sane adult with a fairly active imagination, sex life and sense of humour, and that you have had parents or figures resembling parents (there are some people who claim to have been raised by goats) for at least part of your life. If any of the above were, or indeed are, lacking in your world, then I hope you can allow me a little latitude here and there.

Thirdly, I am a man, and so many of my examples and anecdotes herein will be, instinctively, from a male perspective; rest assured, however, I will do my best to incorporate the female point of view as well. If you are gay, please do not be offended if large sections of this book completely pass you by. I am, in an unprejudiced manner, talking of 'hetro' marriage. But with a little imagination, you should be able to apply most examples to your own orientation.

And finally, I am rescinding your rights to sue me should anything happen to your marital status once you have finished reading this work. There are some bare truths contained in these pages that some of you might react strongly to: what you hold in your hands right now is rather powerful, and sadly we live in a litigious culture, so I must be on my guard.

If you are already married, well…it's too damn late to take my initial advice anyway; but I hope you will enjoy and learn from it all the same. And yes, I am perfectly aware that *some* marriages work quite satisfactorily. Good for you. Yawn!

Whether you are married or unmarried, this is your chance to be different, to be an individual unaffected by the pressures of the society and the people around you.

My ultimate message: be yourself, not the person that everyone else thinks you should be.

And to the mothers, the wives and the girlfriends who have picked up this book thinking that it is aimed solely at men, let me assure you that I am a firm believer in the strength of the woman, so do not judge *this* book by its cover.

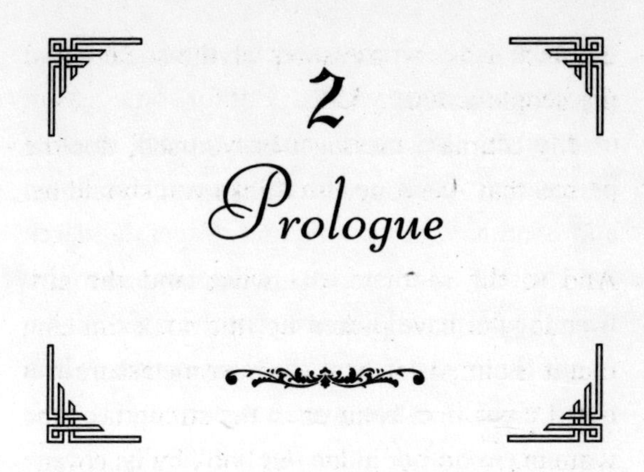

2 Prologue

It has been a long time since I thought of marriage as a serious proposal, and because of this I am a far happier and more relaxed individual. Think about it: how many people do you know who spend too much time running around worrying about *who* they are going to marry, *when* they are going to marry, *where* they are going to marry, and worst of all, *if* they are going to marry? Are you one of them? Probably: I used to be too. But do not fret; there is hope for you yet. Please read on.

There has been a time in all our lives when we have thought, 'Yes, this is it... this is the one I could marry!' and yet whether we were seven or seventy-seven, we have later discovered that we were sadly wrong, and have walked away, dejected and disappointed. But for some reason or another, after such a major setback most of us have got back up, brushed ourselves down and continued our manic and desperate search for 'the one'. It seems we are determined to live with the perpetual illusion that the right person is out there, just round the next corner – in a bar, a club, an office, even a supermarket – and that once we locate them, we will finally acquire true and lasting happiness.

Hold on a second. What did I just write? Was it that we can only find 'true and lasting happiness' with *another person*? Well, I am ashamed of myself for even suggesting such a ridiculous notion! And yet you and I know that, deep down, we all share the same delusion that it is only 'someone else' who can complete the complicated jigsaw of our lives and bring us contentment. Unfortunately, this someone else will only completely complicate the complicated jigsaw even further. Rest assured, however, we hold this fallacy through no fault of our own: it is instilled in us as little children.

3 Childhood

Our whole childhood is geared towards us finding the 'ideal lifetime partner': from what our parents say, to what our school teaches, to what our society shows, to what our inherited religion dictates. But to my mind, this is all nothing but a 'mis-education'. From day one, we are led up the wrong path: the path of dependence instead of independence, insecurity instead of security. We are encouraged to need *another*, expect *another* and be desperate about *another*. But such wants and feelings only lead to disaster. The fact is, 'If expectation is the mother of disaster, then desperation is the sister.'

Do you remember when you were small? Now think back to those occasions when you used to casually natter to your parents about what was going on in your life: you know… about your friends, which girls or boys you fancied, how ravishing your biology teacher was, and how you had just sneaked a peak up your English teacher's skirt. Well, more often than we now care to remember, these informal, and seemingly inconsequential, chats always meant something much more to our parents. Yes, they represented opportunities for them to impart their pitiful wisdom and worldview; and some reference to marriage – a subliminal, manipulative and insistent little comment – would invariably creep in somewhere. A phrase that still rings in my ears to this day is, 'When you get married… blah, blah, blah'. This is the phrase that initiates all expectation, and all the proceeding desperation, divorces and disaster. It is never, and I mean never, ever, *ever*, '*If* you get married…?' Well, not from where I was standing anyway. It was always, '*When*…', as if there was simply no doubt about the matter. Marriage was presented as something vital and inevitable.

And herein lies the reason why we are blameless in our nagging need to have a lifetime partner. As Philip Larkin famously wrote:

> They fuck you up, your mum and dad.
> They may not mean to, but they do.
> They fill you with the faults they had
> And add some extra, just for you.

Need I say more? It is not, I repeat not, our fault, but the fault of our parents, their parents, their parents' parents.

Now the majority of them do not do it intentionally. It's just the way it is, what they do as parents: they fill us with all their own faults and expectations. And likewise, when we become parents ourselves, we will no doubt do the same. Hence, it becomes a perpetual cycle of 'mis-education', passed on from generation to generation – like a bad temper or nervous twitch – something that few of us comprehend, let alone think about.

These flaws and wishes are embedded so deep within us, in our subconscious, that they manifest themselves in all our behaviour. When we start to play games at a young age, we often begin with 'Doctors and Nurses' (undoubtedly the best way to fondle the opposite sex), and we end up playing... yes, you've guessed it, 'Mummies and Daddies'. Why, oh why, are we already on the slippery slope of 'companionship desperation' at such a young age? Again, we need look no further than Larkin.

Though I blame our parents for the majority of this brainwashing and our subsequent insecurities – for it is *they* who created, nurtured and controlled us – I must also point the finger at society in general (especially our teachers and peers), and its abundance of aphorisms (adages of truth, my arse!) and proverbs. The saying 'Two's company' is just one such example. This little maxim creates a need in all of us: it spells out, emphatically, that it is better not to be alone. We must have *someone else* – a partner, a playmate – in order to be happy. How many times have you heard these lethal words uttered? A thousand times, I bet, from the moment you were born. And this damn adage surely breeds insecurity, albeit subliminally, which then cultivates neediness, that finally produces… yes, right again: marriage!

Even at school, we were instructed to hold hands with our nearest classmate when we went outside the grounds and collectively assume the 'crocodile formation': talk about making us feel like we should be with someone! It is as if we were judged, right from the off, completely incapable of looking after ourselves. And they, the teachers, told us that it was for our own good, our own protection. To a certain extent, they were right: it is, of course, more difficult to run away if someone is clutching your hand. And so, you see, the notion of the ball and chain was introduced to us at a very young age, in subtle, metaphorical guises. We were pushed towards the companion way of thinking; that we needed someone to be there, always by our side. And before we knew it, we had lost our natural ability to stand alone.

Throughout our childhood, our innate independence was undermined; we were constantly meddled with and monitored, pushed towards companionship. We were either watched obsessively by our parents, molly-coddled and irritated by a baby-sitter, or forced to endure a string of school friends whom we did not really like but ended up counting as good friends simply because we did not know anyone else. So, when we were finally left to our own devices, we passed the time inanely and reluctantly; we watched TV, played video games, and then tried to poke out the neighbour's cat's eyes with a stick.

Look, my point in all this is that we were never encouraged to spend quality time with ourselves. And so, once we got bored of TV, video games and the cat, our parents responded not by encouraging us to use our imagination or by planting constructive ideas in our head, but with a quick and easy phone call to 'rent-a-friend'. To me, it's a bit like chocolate: you don't miss it until you've had it; but once you have had it, you crave it. And companionship is the same. We were just fine being with our family and friends every so often, but no, this was not enough for our parents. They insisted we must be with them and others *all the time*, so much so that when we were finally granted solitude, we could not handle it: we were 'companionship addicts' now, and needed someone to play with, shout at or fight with – incidentally, these are the three key elements of all our future relationships.

So childhood is the time when all the brainwashing occurs: the child's mind is a sponge and soaks up everything. And because we are victims of this wicked propaganda when we are so very young, we see nothing wrong in parading confidently down the aisle years later, as if we know exactly what we are doing. Why do we march so blindly towards 'M'? Well, because we have simply not been given any other option (until now, that is!). And thus when the ring goes on that finger, this is not the time when we finally rejoice, no, but rather the moment when we at last realize what we have *actually* gone and done, what has *really* happened: we have been played for a fool, well and truly handcuffed and suckered.

Don't get me wrong: I think it is wonderful to have friends, hang out and chat, be loved and cherished, but it is the way we are convinced as children to have 'expectations of eternity' – that any 'real' and 'good' relationship ought to last forever – where things start to turn sour. We are made to feel that any friendship must be all or nothing; we should feel guilty unless we are in constant touch with a friend; a good friend is someone we are with, and talk to, all the time. Time and distance are portrayed as enemies, to be vanquished. And yet any friendship we have that really means something to us is less about how much actual time we spend with this person and how close by we live, but more about what he or she is actually like. And let us be realistic, most of those friends or lovers we have had with whom we initially spent every waking hour were never around for long; our relationships with them withered as fast as they had first bloomed.

There is nothing wrong with a child, and in turn an adult, who wants to be alone. Children are victims of a lot of pointless interaction. A child who likes to spend time alone, who is able to amuse him or herself, who does not need to be surrounded by people or toys the whole time, who is an individual with a strong will and an independent mind, should be congratulated not chastised; respected not scorned.

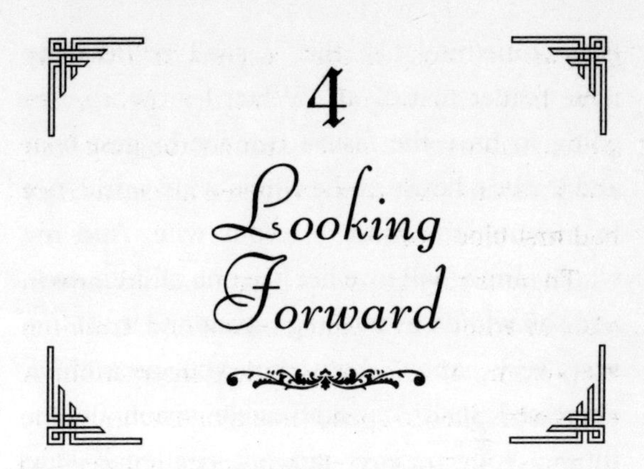

4 Looking Forward

So, here we are, this young little innocent, just five or six years old, in a world of beauty, excitement and endless possibilities with our whole life ahead of us (remember, this was a time when reaching eighteen was an aeon away and hitting twenty-five was simply inconceivable), and yet even here, we are trapped into thinking that unless we end up married by the time we're thirty-five, with a family and a stable career, we have not fully realized our potential and have thus, in some way, failed. What a terrible burden to place on a small child. We should be ashamed of ourselves! But we're not.

Parents actively encourage their child's imagination to take flight, and the ensuing fancy goes something like this. I shall address my male reader first of all. 'When I grow up, I'm going to have the fastest car, the biggest boat and the best house in the whole wide world, not to mention the most gorgeous wife. And my whole family will love her like one of their own, and she will do everything I want and make me very, very happy.' And when you, as a child, expressed such an implausible vision of the future, your parents did not challenge your fantasy and urge you to confront reality, no, they actually nurtured your severely misguided beliefs with 'oohs' and 'aahs' and encouraged all your lavish pronouncements with comments such as, 'Yes, you will have all this one day, as long as you behave yourself now.' They clearly lied, and we believed them.

But, for your parents, feeding you such a grotesque and ruinous illusion was easier than having to articulate the difficult truth of marriage: that your future wife will have a character, and set of ambitions, of her own. And yet, when your parents first planted the chimera, such potential sources of conflict were simply dismissed. 'There is someone out there who is perfect for you, who will complete your life,' they said, anything to steer you into the world they had imagined for you, and more importantly, for themselves. What drivel! It is beyond the bounds of decency that children are subjected to this drivel, and yet, more likely than not, they will regurgitate it when they become adults too.

Now to address my female reader, you have probably been subjected to one of two schools of thought. Either that all men are self-centred bastards who are only after one thing, so stay away, or that (and this is the more prevalent, rose-coloured view) *when* you marry, you will be the most adored, respected, loved and cherished wife in the whole wide world... ever.

Of course, both are completely wrong. If the first were right, then the entire female species would by now be one giant legion of lesbians (hmm), and if the second were right, all women would be happily married (ha!).

If you have been subjected to the former school of thought, your parents have pushed you into thinking that marriage is a man-made career move that cannot benefit you in the slightest; in which case you decide it is your duty as a girl to find a man, marry him and try to change him, fail miserably (because people don't change), and simply end up proving that your parents were right all along.

Or, alternatively, you who have been fed the latter viewpoint – with all its wonderful optimism – and swallowed it hook, line and sinker. So sure are you that your parents are right about marriage – this noble and great family institution, which is both respectable and dignified – that you go in search of it, find a man and marry him, but then discover that he does not adore, respect, love and cherish you as he is meant to, so you try to change him and fail (because people don't change), and so what follows is not never-ending marital bliss but rather a messy and vulgar divorce with all the characteristics of a raging battle. And by the end of it all, you must finally accept that marriage is not this remarkable and immaculate thing after all.

And so, as children, the majority of us are herded blindly towards a life of 'honeycombed unreality', and we perpetually seek out this honeycomb in our adulthood, so sure are we that it exists because we have been consistently told it does. Well, this book is intent on stripping away all this unreality and giving you some bare-boned reality. But rest assured you will find a surprising amount of honey even here, beneath all the fairytale and fancy. I encourage you to be honest with yourself now... totally honest.

Look around you. How well are other people's marriages *really* faring? We can now access infidelity and betrayal every day and at any time: be it on the front page of a tabloid newspaper first thing in the morning (the marital woes of yet another attention-seeking celebrity); on a trashy soap opera in the afternoon; in a cinema in the evening; or on a radio talk show late at night (another recent divorcee driven to call in at two o'clock in the morning because, plagued by the failures of a marriage, he or she is now suffering from terrible insomnia). And then what about the marriages of people you do know, your work colleagues, your friends, members of your own family? How are these, in truth? And finally look at the course of your own love life thus far...

Now, realize this: that despite all of the above, and despite the following... that most people live in a cesspool of boredom and regret once they are married; that the majority of marriages end in divorce; that even before the inevitable divorce the marriage was a disaster waiting to happen (and everyone could see it); that everyone knows someone who is cheating, or would like to cheat, on their partner (look in the mirror and there they are); that many of us struggle to maintain a relationship for more than a few months; and that life is characterized by change (because this is the only thing that keeps us alive)... still we convince ourselves that it will somehow be different for us (such is the power of our parents' indoctrination) and that we, against all the odds and all the facts that stare us in the face, will find that one person to be with *forever*.

When on earth are we going to finally wake up and realize that the future will not be exactly as we had imagined it? Or should I say, exactly as our parents had imagined it for us? Well, I suggest right now! It's as good a time as any, and could save you a whole lot of pain, anguish and cash!

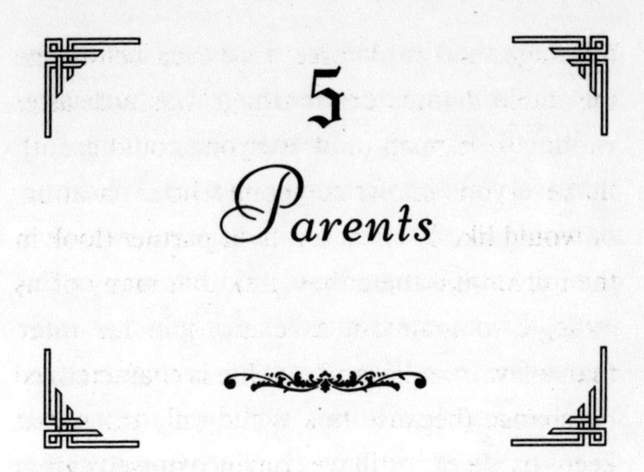

5 Parents

I have already commented on the way parents love to place, in children's minds, the idea that marriage is as innate as breathing, and I shall now expand on the disastrous role parents play in making children feel inadequate unless they find a mate for life.

It is a ridiculous but all-too-prevalent facet of childhood that children consider their parents the most flawless people on earth: they are supremely wise, intelligent and competent (and if children are lucky, loving as well), hence everything they say and do represents the pinnacle of truth and wisdom. It is only when children grow older and reach adulthood that they finally develop a critical faculty... and can at last see their parents for what they accurately are... utterly imperfect like the rest of humanity.

We all know by now that being an adult is hardly a state of perfection. Rather, we are in many ways still as confused as when we were children, still struggling to find our way in the world. Every day is another day gone, another day away from the dreams we might never achieve, and if we have achieved them, well then we are more than likely striving to reach greater heights still, driven by a perpetual state of restlessness and dissatisfaction. And here is the dilemma: when we are children, we look up to our parents as the ones who know best, but when we are adults, afflicted by world-weariness and fear, we hope that any mistakes we made when growing up will not be repeated by our own children. And yet there is a rather lamentable aspect to all this: it is more than likely that our children will nevertheless do just as we did. What we try and get them to avoid, they will solicit and do regardless. Yes, there is a tragic fatalism at work here.

Rather than parents admitting to themselves, and to their children, that marriage is more complicated and challenging than de-boning a fish with their tongue, they actively encourage their children to believe that marriage is an ideal state for them, and everyone. What this, of course, essentially equates to is, 'Everyone else does it, so you should too!' And it is this tragic logic of consensus that has screwed up more adults and more children than drugs or alcohol could ever hope to. What parents really mean when they utter these words of common consent to their children is, 'I screwed up, but I just cannot admit it, and so you will have to suffer my fate too.'

Now please think about this strangest of facts. We are all aware that most marriages are particularly hard work, full of resentment, packed with disagreements, and often end in divorce. So why, oh why, do the majority of parents encourage their offspring to marry? It would seem that parents devote a lot of their time to ensuring that their children do not make obvious mistakes. They want the best possible future for them, and so strive, first, to give them the best advice they can, and second, to teach them how to do things the best possible way. And yet they do not employ such endeavours when it comes to the issue of marriage. Let me be frank, railroading your child towards a doomed marriage hardly constitutes the best counsel and instruction. In fact, it's irresponsible and cruel, and is probably verging on child abuse as well!

And this 'railroading', well it comes in numerous guises, both subtle and heavy-handed. There are the 'goo-goos' and 'gaa-gaas' that we are bombarded with in the cot and playpen; these inane and meaningless words are simple yet advanced forms of marriage propaganda: they nurture in us a dire need for constant attention and affection from a very young age. And then there are the more blatant attempts to coerce us into marriage.

I address the male reader now. I am sure when you were little there was probably a time when you played with one particular girl on a regular basis either because you fancied her or just liked her (yeah, right!), and when the two of you finally finished playing and left the playground, there would unfailingly be some wisecracking parent who would utter something along the lines of, 'You two look like such a lovely couple. Do you think you're going to get married one day?' Remember this? Well, I mean, come on…what a bloody ridiculous question to ask two four-year-olds! What makes this enquiry even more aggravating is that the parent who posed it probably despised their spouse (who had been consistently unfaithful for the past five years), had a lover of their own and desperately wanted a divorce (in fact had done so since the third year of marriage), yet *still* had the gall to ask *you* and another four-year-old to make a life-altering decision that was not even legal for another twelve years.

Let me offer one more example of parental pressure prior to concluding my rant. Do you remember how awful you felt around the time of school reports – all the worry you went through, sometimes for no reason, sometimes for good reason? I assume you do. Then you might remember the occasion when your parents told you off for not working hard enough. They sat you down and said that if you did not get your head down from now on, you would be gated: yes, you would lose certain fundamental freedoms. Now this was, of course, in itself, hard enough to accept, and though they made every effort to make it sound fair, it clearly was not, but you listened earnestly in spite of this, and pretended to agree with everything they said. However, what you did not realize was that there was more to come: the next threat was to be a whole lot more serious; the one that really got you worrying, the one that made you vow to yourself that you would indeed work harder after all. And this is how it went: 'You have to do well at school,' they said. 'Why?' you asked. 'Because if you don't, you'll never get good qualifications, and then you won't get a good job, and *then* you won't be able to support your spouse and kids.' God, now you were just riddled with anxiety. Yes, this was brute, incontestable adult logic: no arguments, no questions, no doubts. You simply had to work harder to reach your destiny, the destiny assigned to you at birth: marriage and children. That was that!

But hold on a minute, there was a valid response to your parents' threats, which involves free will and individuality, two things we often forget we have, and if spoken by you, it would have gone something like this: 'Excuse me, but who said I want to have a spouse and kids?' Of course most of us never say this, or even think it, because by this stage in our development we have been successfully brainwashed: according to our now skewed logic, marriage is as important as eating, and family life is as much a certainty as death; you are not told that family life will probably *lead* to your death... but by then, you will probably be grateful for the peace and quiet anyway!

Thus parents, by promoting the ideal of marriage so loosely – speaking its name at any available opportunity and using its future non-occurrence or failure in their child's life as a means of discipline and censure – encourage their child to associate his or her future with this ultimate ending, and so those relationships which are unlikely to result in marriage must be dismissed with immediate effect: it is all about finding a mate to tie the knot with.

Hence, all roads lead to the altar. And no matter how many times we falter along the way, and no matter how many times we are unfaithful (let me tell all you blind and naïve men out there, that no matter what you think or hope, women do it far more successfully than men – ever slept with a married woman? They just hide it better than us!), we have become so hell-bent on marriage that we convince ourselves of its sanctity and tell ourselves that we will change once we have taken those sacred vows. Wakey, wakey! Come on, let's just accept it... most of our parents, if not divorced, have been unfaithful at least once and probably think about it more often than you care to imagine. Now, do you really want to marry someone knowing that they are probably going to sleep with someone else? Didn't think so.

Do not misunderstand me – marriage can work, albeit rarely, but it is incredibly laborious and unfulfilling work, and most people simply do not possess either the stamina or the obstinacy to see it through. If you have had a flawless marriage, then well done. Liar. I suspect you might be suffering from some kind of delusion. Go see a doctor.

6 Mother

Women are very different from men; mothers are very different from fathers. The key distinction in respect of the latter is the 'instinct' a woman possesses as a parent: maternal instinct is a compelling force!

Let us look first at the relationship between mother and son. Whether a mother is driven to constantly chide *or* fuss over her son, she will convince herself she does this simply because she wants the best for him. Yet, in reality, she does this because she is motivated by a burning need to assert her status as the primary, and if possible *only*, woman in her son's life: Freudian fancy this might be, and yet there is great truth in it. Thus, although outwardly she encourages her son to marry – society demands it – inwardly, she absolutely dreads the day that he announces his engagement.

But it is here where a shrewd son can use this 'maternal dread' to his advantage. He can collude with his mother; allow her to carry on believing that nobody is good enough for him. And in this way, he can remain single, and succeed in breaking the boring cycle of wedding and divorce that society must currently endure.

And now to the very different relationship between mother and daughter: the moment her daughter is born a mother's life is completely taken over, swallowed up, and she proceeds to live through her, to make of her daughter's life what she has not made of her own. And it is rare that her daughter is thankful for these heroic efforts: no, she is more likely to be an ungrateful little brat! Then to make matters even worse for poor mother, her husband also expects to be cared for, pampered and cherished *just because* he is her husband, this is his entitlement: so goes the wayward logic of the institution of marriage.

Perpetually torn between the needs of her daughter and her husband, mother dear must choose where to direct the majority of her energy, and ultimately, she will direct it to you, oh ungrateful one, because you are her blood, her offspring, an innate part of her, and although you may be an ungrateful little brat, you can be sure he is too, and however much she loves your father, he will never be a biological manifestation of her.

This is the doom that confronts you girls, if you choose to marry: the big 'double take'. Not only will your child *take* from you, but your husband will as well. Feel comfortable about this, do you? If you do, then fine – far be it from me to disrupt your perverse little fantasy – but if you do not, then I ask you to confront the reality of your mother's situation right now, and by so doing, look closely at your future prospects.

And so, trying to understand the peculiar and particular teaching habits of a mother is never easy, but be aware that whatever you see in your mother you will, one day, see in yourself, and the probabilities are that you will fall into the life that your mother now has – you will essentially become your mother: such is the power of 'maternal instinct'. Only by using your own 'instinct' can you avoid the trials and tribulations that your mother, and her mother before her, have had to endure.

Oh…and one more thing for my female reader to consider at this juncture: why, if you do decide to marry a man after months or years of courtship, should it be that you have to give up *your* surname – your family history, your individuality – once the ceremony is over, in favour of *his*? And if you then go on to have children, why should they take your husband's name? Did they not come from *you*? And if you then seek a divorce (which, as you can see by now, is highly likely), do you then want *your* children to keep *his* name? You are, after all, their mother. You carried and fed them from the moment they were conceived. Are they not more a part of *you* than *him*? And then once you are divorced, must you then be forced to continually read *his* name all over *their* lives? This is made even more unreasonable by the fact that it will most likely be *you*, not him, who must look after the children post divorce.

Now, I ask all you women to abandon once and for all the notion that marriage will provide you with a better, happier, more fulfilling life because in most cases it simply will not. This is one of the great fallacies! Rather it will nurture a terrible dependency in you: you will be made reliant upon a husband who will more than likely be at work all the time, and when he is at home, will either be hungry, drunk or just plain tired. And so you will be made to feel increasingly unattractive, unappreciated and unloved: the marital union is hardly conducive to passion and romance…

Look, I want you to face up to the sheer horror of 'M'. If you are a divorcee with children, well then hear what I say and help your children to stay happy, free and single. And if you are a single mother who did not marry, well then celebrate your status – you should be proud not ashamed of it (as long as you are not a welfare scam-artist) – and instil the same independence and conviction in your children.

Mothers of the world, 'unite in your apathy' and help us sustain our precious individuality.

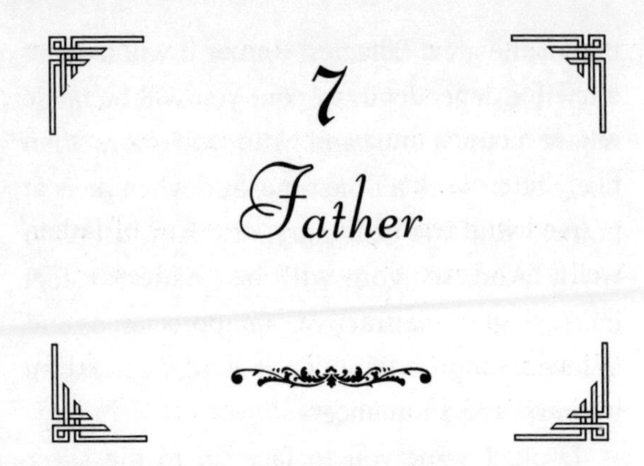

7 Father

Now I must confess at this point – though it is perhaps due to my own father's complete vapidity, or how distant my friends' fathers were, or indeed the prevailing image of the aloof, emotionally reticent and authoritarian patriarch – that I have little to say here.

Save that, in general, there are two types of married fathers: either a self-confessed, unrepentant bastard – a perfect example of why not to marry; or a repressed, housebound bore – also a perfect example of why not to marry.

With regards to the former, his infidelity is inevitable: he should not be chastised for his inability to control his libido, to exercise his powers of seduction. Is this not the natural male state? However, he should be judged for what follows: when his infidelity is exposed, and the entire family is torn apart by terrible rage, bitterness and distrust.

And with regards to the latter type of father, well I have little to say, and neither does he.

What is the difference between a faithful husband and an unfaithful husband?

One gets caught.

8 Only Child

Now that we have considered the effect of parents, let us look at the effect of siblings, or lack of them.

An only child is prone to display certain negative character traits, in particular self-absorption; though unappealing qualities such as this are clearly born out of the child's status as 'the one and only' – the parents' most precious commodity.

Think of those occasions when the parents of a single child must wait with other parents, just beyond the school gates, in order to pick up their child: they are driven to brag incessantly about *their* child's (let us call him 'Little Johnny' for the sake of argument) great achievements.

And yet the need for victory here drives the parents of Little Johnny to spoil him rotten. It is not enough that he keep up with his contemporaries. No, he must surpass them! And so he must be constantly rewarded... and coveted.

In this respect, parents with two or more children have a natural advantage – if victory is not provided by one child then it will hopefully be provided by another – whereas Little Johnny finds himself the victim of a brutal 'all or nothing' philosophy employed by his parents.

At home, away from other children and their parents, Little Johnny is king – the great hero of his own small world – and his doting parents actively nurture this inflated sense of self in him. You see, this is beneficial for them. Why? Well... because Little Johnny now considers himself 'King of the World', he is able to amuse himself for days, weeks, months, even years on end (he can never tire of his immense stature – albeit a superficial one), and thus his parents are granted at least a little space and time, not only from him but also from his dreadful little friends. And furthermore, because he is so full of himself, he needs little instruction and discipline: he is destined to excel at anything he turns his mind to. But consequently, Little Johnny is an arrogant bugger... and damn selfish.

When I was a boy, I had a friend who was an only child and he used to do the following: when he came to my house, he would insist that he have the best gun because he was the guest, and yet when I went to his house, he would still insist that he have the best gun, but this time because he was the host. 'What the hell is all this about?' I used to ask myself then... and I still ask myself now. Well, I can only attribute such unreasonable behaviour to 'only child syndrome'.

Please excuse this brief digression. Back to the matter in hand: let us imagine that we are at home with Mum, Dad and their precious Little Johnny. Mum has just cooked a wonderful breakfast and now finds herself clearing away all the dishes (God only knows why. She not only bought the food but had to cook it and lay the table. And now, despite all that she has done, she is still expected to clear and wash up – such is a wife's prerogative. Dear female reader, please take note!) while Dad lounges on the armchair like a great big sloth, newspaper perched on his round belly, and Little Johnny waits impatiently to be taken shopping again to buy yet more toys (he has far too many already). And as little Johnny asks, 'Can we go *now*?' for the hundredth time, Dad, having finally run out of excuses as to why he should remain bloated and catatonic on the sofa, pipes up with the following: 'So Johnny, which girls at school chased you this week?' And suddenly, toy-shopping is off the agenda and we are off into the realms of, 'When you get married…'

Little Johnny is Mum and Dad's only hope, you see, and if he does not marry, well then he does not procreate…and if he does not procreate, well then he will not give them grandchildren. And this means no anecdotes beginning with either 'When I was young…' or 'In my day, things were different…', no grand parting to the Gates of Heaven, no graveside visits, no remembrance at Christmas, no legacy. Without grandchildren they will be reduced to nothing…*rien*, *nada*, *nichts*, *nechevo*, zilch.

We all know very well that a branch on the family tree which does not continue to grow – sprout yet more branches – is just dead wood, rotten, a damn failure. And such failure is not an option!

So please, spare a thought for an only child: he or she is under considerable pressure from the get-go.

Beware Little Johnny.

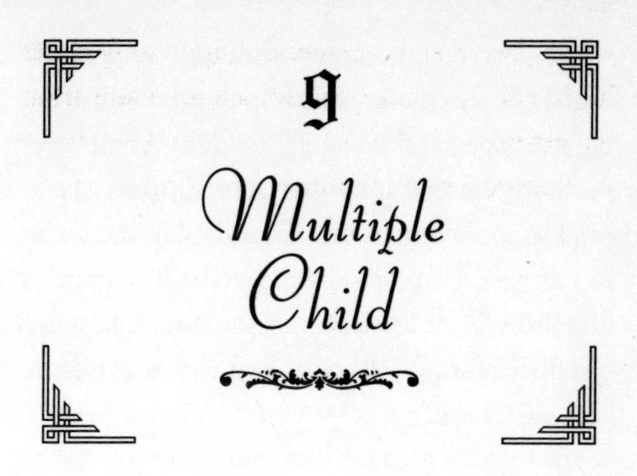

9 Multiple Child

As one of many, one is always up against the many. This is the fate of 'multiple child', the one with siblings.

Let us call our multiple child 'Sarah' and let us suppose that she has four sisters, two older and two younger.

Sarah is also under pressure from the very beginning, and this applies to all aspects of her life: from meal-time to story-time, bath-time to bed-time, high-time to low-time. She must vie constantly for her often stressed and distressed parents' affections and will do almost anything in this pursuit, whether it be bursting into floods of tears for no apparent reason (because there is no reason), volunteering to read bed-time stories to her younger siblings (apparently self*less*, but actually self*ish*!), or even being her parents 'special little agent' (snitch). Whichever method she employs, her motivation is clear (and to some degree understandable): she wants to have *her* share of affection, to be the centre of attention for at least part of the day. And when Sarah reaches adulthood, still she is driven to seek her share.

If we cut through the rigmarole of 'when you get married', to maturity, it can quickly be deduced by a cunning and desperate child (which is what all 'multiple children' are by definition) that to announce an engagement, leading to a marriage, on to a first child and grandchild, will rapidly place 'multiple child' into the coveted and enviable position of 'star child'.

This change of status not only gives 'immediate attention gratification', it also creates long-term importance within the family hierarchy. From the moment the engagement is announced, Sarah becomes the number one topic of conversation, as well as being her parents' principal concern: mission accomplished! Her wedding plans consume not just her parents but her siblings, the whole family. She is all of a sudden granted special treatment: she can change her mind at any time, about anything; she is given more money to prepare for her new married life ('Dear Daddy' even lets her use his credit card); and she is granted a *private* audience with her parents whenever she so desires, away from the close scrutiny of her rival siblings. She never would have received such privileges before, because there was always another 'multiple child' stealing her parents' affections. Now, all of a sudden they are willing to give her anything…and there are no rules, no boundaries; only the limits of her once constrained imagination.

She has also succeeded in beating her two elder sisters to the post. And it must be said, she derives immense satisfaction from this victory: she got there first!

And so to the big day…and Sarah is the apple pie of her parents' eyes, and yet she knows that their devotion will be even greater when she bears them a grandchild. Meanwhile, her eldest sister quietly hopes that she will be next. Marrying second need not be construed as such a failure, she thinks. She might have better weather on her wedding day, yes, and the service might be more beautiful, the speeches more eloquent … and finally, she might be better suited to her husband than Sarah is to hers: her marriage will be stronger, will last longer, she hopes. (Oh God, she really is desperate.)

Please do not dismiss this as appalling cynicism: such sibling rivalry is inescapable! Some of you reading this might insist you are not like this. Let me put it to you that, in all probability, you *are* like this, and what is stopping you acknowledging this grim fact about yourself is your simple dread at exploring the darker regions of your heart.

You see, we all need our share of attention, affection, praise and love.

Beware brothers and sisters.

10 Children's Toys

Toys are all about having possessions that are *yours* and no one else's. You might lend one to a friend for an hour or two, but even in someone else's hands, it still remains *your* property. And if a toy is not yours but someone else's, then you typically want it for yourself; such is the instinctive drive for ownership.

All children have a favourite toy, whether it is a teddy bear, a train, a car or a game, and they also have a favourite play figure – be this a Barbie doll or an Action Man – which they cherish beyond compare, in fact so much so that its loss or harm causes the child (and consequently the parents) untold distress.

But we have to wonder why such tears and tantrums occur over an inanimate playmate. Well, put simply, it is because the child finds it highly desirable: the child can possess it entirely, and it is utterly subservient to the child's every whim. This object, and the behaviour it inspires, become the barometer by which we can judge the future.

For girls, Barbie fulfils all the dreams of romantic love, of being desired, of being glamorous, of being sexy...a fully fledged woman (but without nipples or pubes). She is a figure to aspire to, a vision of consummate femininity. Barbie is their friend, their ideal – she turns heads but remains unaffected by the attention (because she is dumb). She was designed not just for girls' pleasure but for boys' gratification as well: she is pretty, slim, and for want of a better word, chic. However, boys keep their hands off her for fear of being called 'girlie', and this is just fine for Barbie and her friends.

For boys, Action Man fulfils all the fantasies of what it means to be a 'real man' (men realize only as they grow older that the definition of 'real' is fraught with subjectivity): he is square-jawed, broad-shouldered, carries a scar and wears combat trousers; he looks 'lived in', the 'silent but strong' type, and most importantly, he alone knows how to work all those complicated instruments needed to locate and destroy the enemy. He is a mini superhero who never dies, and never has to go to the hairdresser. And yet to the immense disappointment of every man, woman and child who encounters him, he has no genitalia whatsoever! Boys maintain that he is so busy saving the world that he simply does not have time for a girlfriend (not that he could satisfy one anyway). But his absence of generative organs does not stop him being 'cool' (if a little peculiar) to boys and intriguing (if a little unfulfilling) to girls: they might have been young and innocent but could never resist sneaking a peek down his pants, only to discover that there was nothing down there!

Barbie and Action Man offered us wonderful fantasies when we were children, and we aspired to be just like them. However, they showed us that even perfection is flawed – Barbie had no character and no holes, and Action Man caused every child in the world to sigh with worry and disappointment when he was naked: little boys wondered what theirs would look like when they grew up, but Action Man gave them no clue; and little girls, who were hoping to find out what future excitement lay in store for them, were sorely disappointed. And so, we rejected them in favour of other idols.

And this is a metaphor for all future relationships: *it is the things which are hidden in the beginning that cause the most distress when revealed.*

We were initially prepared to endure the disappointment of discovering the truth about Barbie and Action Man; but over time, our affections wilted and we found ourselves seeking out other playmates. The same can be said for our adult relationships. We try and maintain the fantasy of Barbie and Action Man, and in so doing, we refuse to acknowledge the shortcomings of the man (he might have a penis but he is overweight and a bit of a coward) or woman (she might be intelligent but she is fast losing her looks and is rather demanding) we intend to marry.

You see, no matter how great our toy seems to us at the time, we *will* eventually become tired of it, and so will go in search of another toy. History does repeat itself.

Marriage is driven by our need for possession: we tell ourselves that it is only once we are married that we will have a proper hold of someone, that he or she will be ours for eternity. And yet just like our favourite toy when we were children, we spend the first few days, months, perhaps years, doting on our new husband or wife and relishing our exclusive contract with them, but then slowly become bored and wish we were no longer bound by such a restrictive agreement, and were free again. And yet we have made those blessed vows ... we are bound now ... and simply do not know what to do ...

Why can't we find happiness and harmony within ourselves? Why must we think that such emotional states are only attainable with a husband or wife? I advocate lovers, companions and friends, yes ... such relationships are vital ... but they need not conclude in marriage: for then they become something else altogether.

We were never contractually committed to Barbie or Action Man, and so when we wanted to move on, letting go was easy, and the memories we have of them are still fond even now. Why cannot our adult relationships follow such an enlightened course? Perhaps if we changed our attitudes, they would.

Our lives are characterized by change – the very essence of existence – so should we not allow ourselves the freedom to live according to *this* dictum rather than the crumbling dictum of marriage?

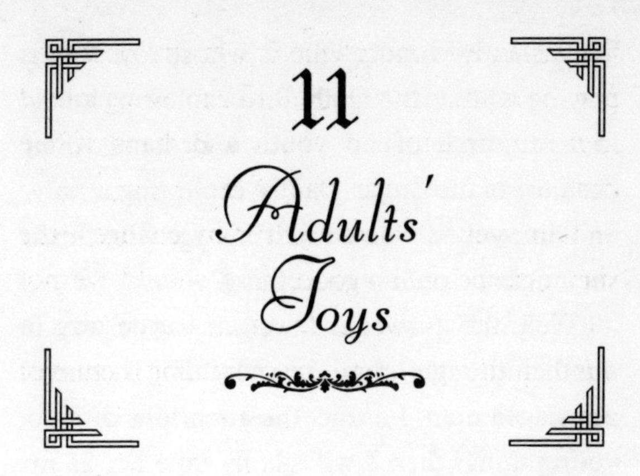

11 Adults' Toys

By the time we reach adulthood, we have, hopefully, discarded Barbie and Action Man in favour of a far more interesting though rather more complex play figure (a real human being); while at the same time we are still haunted by the desire to act out our childhood fantasies. For the purpose at hand, I shall categorize these figures of adult play into three compartments: the opposite sex, possessions (not including the opposite sex) and sex toys.

Let us start with the opposite sex. I think it is safe to say that men and women often play with each other as if they were toys. The familiar image that reinforces this notion is of the Sugar Daddy with a Dolly Bird on his arm.

We instantly wonder who is whose toy, who is playing who. Is the Dolly Bird exploiting an old fool in search of his youth and some young flesh, or is the Sugar Daddy exploiting a naïve and dim-witted woman half his age who thinks she might be onto a good thing?

Well, the answer is never clear one way or another, though let me say now that if, when I am an old man, I attract the attentions of a hot young thing, then I will gladly take her as my Dolly Bird (there are certain opportunities in life that are simply too good to pass up!), and if I happen to be wealthy as well (there is little chance she would find me attractive if I were poor), then she will most likely happily take me as her Sugar Daddy: there is only so much harm an old man can do, and I will leave her a few million to be getting on with once I'm dead. (What a dreamer!)

Men and women using each other is nothing new, but the question now is, 'Who gains the most?' Well, I would have to say, 'Men, of course!' Allow me to clarify. Imagine a small boy and a small girl trying to look at each others bits and pieces:

Boy: 'Look what I've got!' (pointing to his penis, excitedly).
Girl: 'Yeah, but with one of *these* (staring at her vagina), I can have as many of *those* as I like!'

And there we have it! Girls have the power. Any girl, if sly enough, can devour a man before she gives him what he wants! Thus, if a man does succeed in seducing a woman, he has done so against great social and biological odds: it is easier for a woman to 'get laid' than it is for a man. And hence, he has gained the most.

Let us return to our Sugar Daddy. Okay, so before he marries Dolly Bird, he has gained the most: he is a winner! And yet as soon as he marries her, his status plummets. From being the old 'player' and philanderer, who has at least some sort of grip on reality, he suddenly becomes the fool, the laughing stock, the incontinent old plonker who is taking it all a little too seriously and is being taken for a ride (he actually thinks that she would still love him even if he were a pauper). This does his already shaky image no favours, but he doesn't care because he is so old he cannot hear the sniggering, and then, after just two years of marriage, he drops down dead anyway.

Now it is the woman who has gained the most!

Men must battle with their biology day after day, 'live with the sex maniac inside them', as Kingsley Amis remarked. They have little or no control over their libidos, constantly crave sexual discharge, and need their fragile egos stroked at all times. If you have any doubt about such a view of the male species (I address not only my female reader now, but also my repressed male reader), then I ask you to walk into the next strip club you come across and observe the scene. What you will find is nothing short of embarrassing – men giving away their money simply to gawp at naked women, and if they are in greater need still, handing over even more 'moolah' to have these women lap dance for them; and still, when they are spending literally hundreds of pounds, they are not even allowed to touch any of these women. You see, woman is the master! And yes, men are beholden to their penises. It is sad, but true.

Now let us consider possessions. Here, we are confronted with a man's desperate desire to show that he has more than the next man. This need can, at times, appear quite pathetic, and yet its source is clear enough. Even in this day and age, man still feels the need to prove that he can provide for his mate; not only will his ability to do this empower him, but *her* also: she will be able to stand tall, among her friends and contemporaries, with a wealthy man on her arm. You see, he is well aware of the allure of his glory: it will reflect on the woman that stands beside him, and so make her glorious as well.

Isn't it funny how the man with the *most* houses, cars, yachts and planes also has the *most* beautiful wife? And yet what is even funnier is that the superlative beauty of his wife is not enough for him – he is greedy, never satisfied and must prove himself further – and so he prowls, picking up mistresses along the way. Of course, his beautiful wife knows instinctively what he is up to, searches for proof and finds it, and then rather than leaving him and all his riches (she could, but would stand to lead a less extravagant life on her own), starts to acquire lovers for herself. And so the marriage becomes a loveless sham: he is now repulsed by her because she sleeps with other men, and she by him because it was his inability, first and foremost, to keep his dick inside his trousers that drove her to want and need other men. And though she knows that many men are unfaithful, it is the absence of his love that she finds most intolerable and upsetting. And yet, being his wife, she is now left with little choice: either endure a loveless marriage or suffer a gruelling and bitter divorce.

We must, of course, wonder what would have happened between them had they not got married. Well, I suspect that they would more than likely still love one another now... to some degree at least. For without the guarantee of possession that the institution of marriage provides, they would have been driven to seek out and practise more noble and laudable ways of maintaining a contented relationship with each other. They would not have simply relied upon a ceremony, a piece of paper and a ring or two.

And finally, let us look at sex toys. There are only two things I want say about them. First, if a couple is driven to use them because this is the only damn way that the man and woman concerned can get off on one another, then there is clearly something very wrong in their relationship. However, if a couple uses them because the man and woman are just rather naughty and kinky, and well... like to experiment, then great!

Now, the majority of you who are, at this moment, nodding and grinning to yourselves, sure that you are naughty and kinky rather than just plain bored and frustrated, are probably kidding yourselves. The acid test for your 'naughtiness' and 'kinkiness' is whether you go to S&M parties more than three times a year, *every* year. And if you do not, well then you are in point of fact bored and frustrated, not naughty and kinky.

Oh... and one last thing: if anyone ever finds your sex toys, they will more than likely tell everyone you know. So hide them well!

12 Children as Toys

There is no denying it: children are a *huge* responsibility! They take up unquestionable amounts of time, energy and money; they take years to whip into shape (although it is more often than not a completely different shape to the one intended); and when they finally reach eighteen and begin to become an acceptable asset, they disappear into the great wide yonder to leave the parents wondering whether it was really all worth it? And these common traits of parenthood beg the question, 'Why do we have children in the first place?'

Well, for starters, we have no idea how demanding they are going to be, but unlike other toys, which we only have a limited attachment to, and which can be discarded at a moments notice, a child is a toy that is the ultimate extension of the ego: this is after all what all toys are designed to satisfy.

The ability to procreate is a sign of virility. And over and above 'flashing the cash', the ability to support a large family displays a form of wealth and legitimacy that pure cash cannot. You see, apart from our powerful instinctive drive to procreate, one of the main reasons we have children is that we feel we must leave behind a legacy, our memory must live on. This is the ultimate goal.

To this end, children are nothing more than another toy on the shopping list of life. Just as we must garner an acceptable education or apprenticeship in order to finance the lifestyle which will help us attract a spouse that we are proud to show off; surely we will also aspire to have a child, a continuous extension of ourselves, and a living toy that will instil more pride in our hearts and minds than any house, car or dog.

For humans, it is always about the next best thing, and as the targets are met, we come to realize that to actually produce a toy that is completely and utterly unique, well... that would be the ultimate achievement. And so, there we have it, the best toy in the world is the one that you create yourself. Of course, once we have one, we will always want another.

When the baby is first born, it is the most enchanting, time-consuming and important toy a parent could ever hope for: although it is very demanding and requires an enormous amount of attention, it also offers its parents constant joy and wonder. But with the passage of time, and despite this parental love, the initial feelings of excitement begin to fade. And so, just as when we are children we become bored of the old toy and wish to replace it with a newer version, so the idea of having a new baby becomes an intriguing and delightful (though all too commonplace) idea: a new toy is always more fun than an old one, and well, two toys are surely better than one, both for amusement and status.

And yet it is, of course, inevitable that the parents will experience the same yearning after their second child is born: and so perhaps they will have a third. The desire is never satiated. And despite these constant reminders that humans always want more, newer and different, we still see bad parents breeding yet more disturbed children.

People are also driven to have children in order to 'fit in'. Is it not true that once you are married, the very next question is, 'Will you be having babies soon?' It is as if there are certain requirements we have to fulfil in order to be acceptable, and having children is certainly one of them. To this end, we justify procreation by saying to ourselves, 'So many other people have children that I should have some too. After all, is it not our sole purpose to procreate?!' And to this extent, children fulfil a need that all toys fulfil: they help us feel better about ourselves, under the watchful gaze of everyone else.

Let me illustrate this point. If you are a parent, think carefully about the last time someone asked you whether or not you have a child. You answered, 'Yes, I have a son,' I suspect with a hint of pride, which prompted your questioner to confirm that she has one also. You then went on to exchange basic information about your respective children. This prompted you to tell a story about something your son did, and you could not resist a bit of poetic licence here. But when she narrated a story about her child, which made him sound far more sweet and intelligent than yours – she was rather more liberal with her use of hyperbole – you were compelled to think of another event in your son's life that portrayed him as *even* sweeter and *more* intelligent than hers. And so a flurry of anecdotes followed, batted back and forth like a highly competitive ball game, each more ridiculous than the one before, until they no longer contained any semblance of truth.

Now I am sure you have found yourself caught up in such one-up-manship; and you might, afterwards, have chastised yourself for indulging in something so utterly foolish and petty, yet you nevertheless felt compelled to participate in it. It is as if you somehow believed, while in the midst of it, that by asserting your child's worth you were asserting your own; your child became nothing more than a commodity to you, a physical manifestation of your powers. Christ, if you had not been arguing about whose son was more impressive, you would have been arguing about whose car was faster!

And so, as time passes, these toys, I mean these children, grow up and leave home. Different toys must now be found to fill the void: alcohol maybe ... or cars ... perhaps even a new spouse? Take your pick.

13 Pop Songs

Let us move away from toys now and consider something else altogether more subtle yet no less significant: pop songs. You may wonder what on earth these have to do with marriage; well, it is my view that they are one of the biggest culprits driving us towards the dreaded institution.

Pop songs speak in countless tongues and guises about the ins and outs, ups and downs, rights and wrongs of relationships. They are instrumental in affecting our state of mind; they strike a chord in our heart; they make us feel…

But, I wonder, did pop songs make us melancholic or did melancholy make pop songs? Ingeniously sculpted by a bunch of songwriters, pop songs are designed to exploit that part of the human psyche which is weak, needy and unrealistic... which believes that 'the one' is out there somewhere, just waiting to be found.

We have all heard a song and thought, 'Yes, that's me... that's exactly what I'm going through at the moment!' Whether it was because we had just ended a relationship, started a relationship, had an argument, felt true love, loved long distance, or never loved at all; that song gave us a memory, and because of the memory we felt melancholic, and then lonely... we wished we were with someone, building a relationship, a future, which might ultimately lead to... (oh no)... marriage. Hang on a second: where the hell did all *this* come from? All that happened was that I heard that damn song. Such is the power of pop music. Take note.

A pop song has the capacity to arouse great self-pity. It tugs at our heart-strings, it jerks our chain, it twitches our brain, and it makes some fat, emotionless, executive tosser very rich; and to top it all off, it sends us helplessly flailing into neediness and beyond.

And this is the reason that pop songs merit special mention as devious traps to be aware of in marriage avoidance.

14 Films and Fairytales

Compared to a pop song, a film or fairytale works on a far more conscious level: you have to actually stop what you are doing and concentrate on the story at hand. Thus, whereas a pop song is a 'subconscious marriage programmer' (I assure you this is not about to turn into a work of science fiction), a film or fairytale is a 'conscious marriage programmer'. Life is presented to us in soft focus: characters must overcome certain odds, but ultimately they *will* 'live happily ever after'. The myth of the movies and the perfection of fairytales are most definitely to blame for the way we behave within, and without, our relationships.

From early childhood, we are fed fairytales that give us a false perception of our future. Whether a poor little rich girl, or just plain poor, the story of Cinderella is every girl's fantasy: Prince Charming rescuing Cinderella from her sad and grim little world, declaring his undying love for her, then whisking her away on his white stallion to a loving and perfect future. But, in reality, what begins as an innocent fairytale causes a neurosis that develops into a living nightmare for most women; and then, by association, it becomes the same for most men.

For men, there is always the need to be the Knight or the Prince. They spend their lives trying to live up to the expectations that fairytales give to women. But, of course, these expectations only end up leaving men feeling insecure, and women feeling disappointed.

In most relationships, the unrealistic precedent of a perfect partner is maintained for a while, but once the courtship is over (whether before or after the marriage), complacency and familiarity set in and the reality that the Prince is just a human, and the Knight is just a man, end up destroying the fairytale of the 'happily ever after'.

You see, the fantasy is based on the icing on the crumbling cake: this is an apt way to illustrate what happens when a woman realizes her man is not Prince Charming, and her man, in turn, finally gives up trying to be the Knight in shining armour. The cake had a thick layer of icing on it at first; it was beautifully decorated. But now, the woman notices that there seems to be less icing, there are large cracks appearing in it, and some of its adornments have fallen to the floor. And when she looks again, the man is watching as well, as the entire cake crumbles and disintegrates into a messy pile of flour and sugar. Just as sugar is a fattening additive mixed with flour to create something sweet yet superficial, so fantasy was added to reality to create something wonderful yet untrue. Fairy-tales conceal the harshness of reality, as sugar conceals the dourness of flour.

Films are just as powerful as fairytales: we are drawn to them, enchanted by them, so much so that there is one industry dedicated just to *making* them and another dedicated solely to *reporting* on them and yet more are *profiting* from their stories and stars. We have become obsessed with the dreams they offer, and spend billions indulging this infatuation. We lose ourselves in the next romantic comedy, allowing ourselves to believe the illusion that everything will always work out for the best. Even the most macho films have a romantic storyline, as the tough guy and the tough girl finally acquiesce and end up together. And despite all of our own trials and tribulations we are made to feel that we must try to emulate these fictional heroes. Thus, even if we are desperately unhappy in a relationship, we must stick with it: all the heartache will be worth it in the end. *Harry* and *Sally* worked it out, *Danny* and *Sandy* made it! So can we, right? Wrong.

Films are dramatic. They build a dream that we are encouraged to live. We end up confusing escapism for realism and screw ourselves up in pursuit of an unattainable fantasy. Our perception becomes warped, and our ideology becomes drama. And so we embrace the drama in order to give our lives the same meaning as the silver screen, which has held us captive for so long.

These fictional love stories always follow the same pattern: intense love, desperate break-up, then final reconciliation. After the break-up, the hero sits alone looking forlorn. Then we cut to the heroine: she is also alone, and looks equally dejected. And yet we are led to believe that both of them need this time to themselves to finally realize how much they actually love one another. This period of condensed sadness never lasts too long: it is Hollywood after all. And so in the following scene, they are reunited... forever.

Now the reality is, of course, rather different. Firstly because there is nothing more unattractive than a sappy human, and secondly because once the trust is broken, it will never be the same again. Never, ever. So although people get back together, it is based on a fear of the unknown and an inability to confront their solitude. They will never recapture what they had, and will always be skirting around the real issues in order to avoid more confrontation. The relationship is now a lie, waiting to be uncovered. Again.

When will we accept that love is finite and the very idea that it can last forever is an impossible dream? Do not think that your life should be like the narrative of a film and do not try to make it a film: we do not need drama to make our lives worthwhile and fulfilling. When one love affair ends, another one will begin, and this is an excitement a film can never give you. Embrace life for what it is. Embrace love for as long as it is good. Embrace this element of change. Remember that a film comes to a finite conclusion, and life does not. Let me repeat that – a film ends, but real life does not. So please do not confine yourself to the Hollywood ending; the idea that true happiness can only be found with one person is not only ridiculous, it is dangerous.

Do not ever confuse real life with a film, or reality with a fairytale – it will be your downfall.

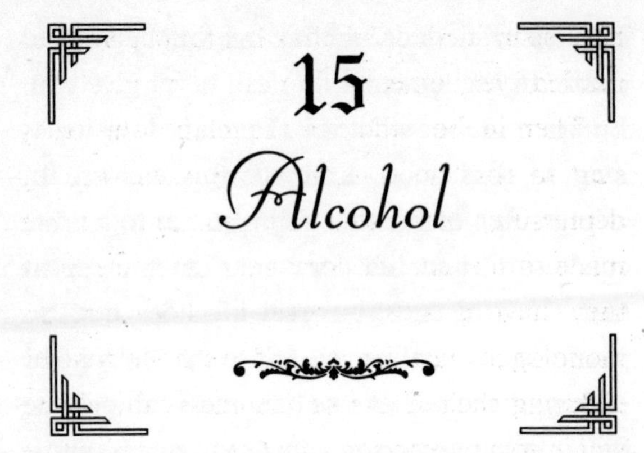

15 Alcohol

Alcohol has the ability to be a very big player in the marriage game – before, during and after.

We are all aware that booze is often responsible for impeding and skewing our judgement. It can affect any relationship at any stage, be it at the beginning, in the middle, or at the end. Any relationship built on 'alcohol-induced happiness' is always going to overflow with problems. Allow me to demonstrate.

At the beginning, when we have just met someone, we think they are perfect because they are so much fun to be with, so happy and carefree: and yet it is drink that has made them so good to be around, and the few nights we have spent with them thus far, they have been razzled every time.

Then in the middle of the relationship, they start to confide in us, revealing their (usually depressing) innermost thoughts, and we are made to feel special because of this: we think they have reserved these painful, drunken monologues just for us, and we hope that by enduring their hours of inebriated drivel, we will in some way contribute towards their future development. And we then go on to tell ourselves – brimming with hope and romantic idealism – that we can cure their sadness, yes, because love conquers all. However, what actually happens is that we cannot cure them, either because they do not want to be cured, or because they are convinced they do not need to be cured, and even though we do everything we can to help them, they never thank us because they are so damn drunk and self-centred.

By the end of the relationship, we find that we resent them whenever they are drunk (which is most of the time), and yet end up getting just as drunk (if you can't beat 'em, join 'em) because we now have no other way of relating to them. There finally comes a point when we simply cannot carry on this way and must break the cycle.

Let us return to our former subjects, Johnny and Sarah: they have been together three years now and are accepting of each other, warts 'n' all. The two of them have mentioned marriage before, and they have heard all the passing quips from friends and relatives about 'Isn't it time you two tied the knot?', but so far that is it: it has been kept firmly in the world of ideas, something which they might want to do 'one day'.

But tonight, Johnny has been drinking and thinking: he is feeling rather unsure about work, his best friend got married last year and is due to have his first child very soon (Johnny has been stewing over whether he should follow his lead), and Sarah... well she has been less attentive to him lately (he worries that she might be going off him). In short, he is not happy at the moment, feels unsure about a number of areas in his life, and needs security. And so, he suddenly decides that he must take the plunge and pop the question: this will solve at least two of the above concerns.

Of course it is going to take some more Dutch courage. And so, the Dutch courage is consumed, and all of the passing quips about 'Isn't it time...?' swell to the forefront of Johnny's mind, transfer to his tongue, and out slurs the fate-decreeing question, 'Will...you... marry...me?'

Sarah cannot believe it at first. His question was so spontaneous: it just seemed to come from nowhere, as if even *he* was not quite sure what he was asking. And yet she is very excited by it, tells Johnny she loves him, but asks for just a few days to make her decision (as if a period of forty-eight hours will provide the necessary clarity). And so she goes on to discuss his proposal with all her family and friends – the majority of whom tell her to say, 'Yes, yes!' (Of course their enthusiasm has nothing to do with the fact that, first, they are married themselves, and second, they possess neither the courage nor the conviction to tell her to do otherwise.) And so, even before Sarah has told them that she will accept Johnny's proposal, they are telling her what ring to get and where she should go for her wedding dress. This is the conspiracy of the majority: before she has even made her decision, whoops, it has been made for her.

Hence, a situation that could have been avoided arises from an alcohol-induced moment. And by now, we all know the statistics.

Alcohol has an amazing ability to cause us to say things that we normally hold close to our hearts. Words, tears, actions and emotions which can be held down quite easily when sober have an uncanny habit of slipping out when one is alcoholically influenszszd! It's almost as if the one thing you shouldn't say, the one thing you keep telling yourself not to say, the dirty word, the rude joke, the forbidden proposal, will unexpectedly shoot out.

The wedding is sometime, someplace, somewhere, who cares? And after this initial stupor of honeymoon bliss is over, and the reality comes to light – marriage does not change things – what should be done? Drown your sorrows, drink, argue, divorce. Deal. Done. DivorcedDepressedDesperate. Drunk. Dead.

And the moral of the story: don't drink and propose. We all have to deal with the aftermath; and it is boring and unoriginal – like a drunkard.

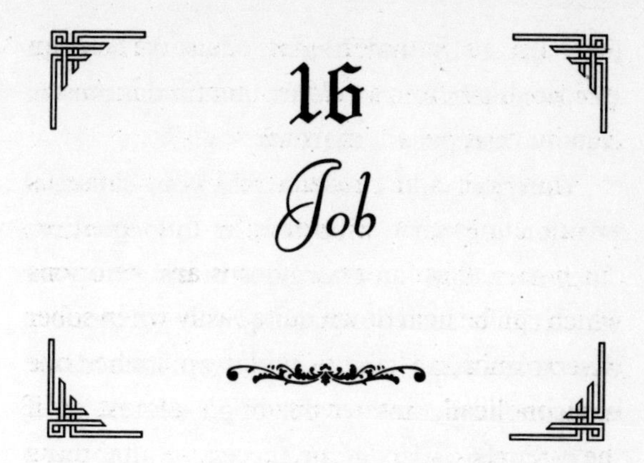

16 Job

Even a job can be incorporated into all things 'marital': it determines income, income is money, money is power, and power is desirable. The better the job the better the income, the better the income the more possessions, the more possessions the bigger the impression, the bigger the impression the greater the power, the greater the power the more desirable you become, the more choice you have, the hotter your partner and the more you want to hold onto them.

Of course, the ultimate and most desirable possession is another human being – more than any car, boat, yacht or plane – and the best way to hold onto this possession without the need for bars, balls and chains, chastity belts or electric shocks is... so we are told (in this present state of disrepair)... marriage.

Your job, and consequently your financial position are very important in this equation. They each have an enormous bearing on your standing in society, enabling you to create a desirable image that provides an immediate, exterior attraction to the opposite sex, and, accordingly, assists in the success of attaining a desirable partner, either through the acquisition of possessions (a big house and a fast car) and/or the acquisition of beauty (designer clothes and sumptuous lips). In the realm of all things superficial, we are driven to make ourselves as desirable as possible, in any way possible, in order to acquire the best partner possible.

But none of this happens without a job, whether it's ours or someone else's (a parent's); as long as we have the money, we are one up on the next person, we have the ability to do the things they can only wish for, and now are more attractive to the opposite sex because we have more money to do fun things with. We all want to be more attractive to the opposite sex, because we all want to have more sex!

Let me point out a common phenomenon. Have you ever met someone, thought very little of them, but then become a lot more interested as soon as you heard quite how filthy rich and powerful they were? It is astounding how our attitude to someone can change in this way. And though we should not be proud of this – our sometime fickleness and superficiality – it is nevertheless part of us. We have all recounted to a friend or stranger, usually with immense pride, the occasion when we met someone who had 'this huge yacht, bodyguards, and a helicopter too!' It is as if a small part of us believed that we had acquired some of their wealth and power simply through our brief association with them. If only.

And fame affects us in the same way. We are now obsessed with celebrity, and aspire to be like someone famous, to have what they have. In fact, it is almost as if we have become so infatuated that we believe in 'reflected glory': the more we learn about them, the more we might actually *become* like them. Again, we are afflicted by the same disease of aspiration.

Thus, there can be no doubt that what you do and what you have holds immense power in the modern world. Your job, and how much you earn, can create or destroy you in the eyes of a potential partner. Everyone is bored by accountants, even accountants are bored by accountants; and most people are guilty of glamourizing their lifestyle to friends and strangers in order not to be undesirable.

Hence the majority of us are driven to marry the one with the best job and the most money. The funny thing is that this is true no matter which income bracket one falls into – people marry the best they can get, relative to their financial position and personal status – and then they regret it.

So, get a great job, but be careful what you do with the power. You might find yourself in a self-made trap.

17 First Love

Now the time has come for us to look at the reasons behind our relentless search for a wife or husband, and the pieces of the puzzle that affect this decision. What on earth keeps us going back, time and time again, for more heartache, more pain and more anguish?

Let us begin with our First Love. I mean this in the proper sense, when our heart was truly on the line with someone for the very first time. We, all of a sudden, felt things we had never felt before – a slight queasiness in our belly, a feeling of light-headedness, a heart which seemed to beat faster, a kind of strange euphoria, sometimes accompanied by nervous ticks, hot flushes or even peculiar bowel movements (but hopefully not!) – and these sensations were being driven by someone else, someone we had fallen *in love* with. What made it quite so extraordinary was that the person we loved so vigorously loved us with equal vigour and was experiencing the same sensations as us.

When we reflect on this First Love now, it just sounds like cliché, the kind of thing written about in trashy romantic novels. And yet millions of such novels are read every year because they contain a large element of truth, their readers desperate to re-capture feelings of First Love, if only through fictional characters. There is no denying that such love was wonderful. Even cynical old I must concede this!

Everything had seemed so perfect. This was in part due to the fact that our tolerance level was higher then than it is now, and so little things did not bother us, and if they did, well… we doubted *our* sanity more than we analysed *their* problem. We had no 'relationship barometer' to go by – this was our *first* love – and so we had no point of comparison, no real measure of the success or failure of the relationship, no expectations and no limitations. And so we continued to tell ourselves that we had found 'the one and only' and we continued to live under the perfection of first-love bliss, until...well...it all went wrong, and our love disappeared.

There was no obvious explanation for this, only a gradual build-up of something inexplicable, and then, BANG! It was all gone: the desire, the need, the happiness, the love – everything good just disappeared. The Grim Reaper of all relationships had struck.

It was monumentally demoralizing. We were left flailing around in no man's land, with no man (or woman) and no land. All we knew was how awful it felt – this was the first time we were hit by 'post-relationship distress disorder' – and my God, it hurt so much.

Yet, although it did not feel like there was a clear explanation for this, there was one (and it is always the same one): time – and its passage is life.

Please disregard the claptrap fed to us by relationship counsellors and therapists who talk about finding someone compatible for life: such speak is pure babble, both juvenile and deluded. How is it possible to find such a person if we are constantly changing? They must change with us, in the same way and at the same rate; otherwise, before we know it, this person who was right for us a moment ago no longer is.

And so it is with First Love. Whether it was our choice to end it or theirs made no difference: time had taken its inevitable toll, and we were devastated, left to confront a huge void that not even chocolate could hope to fill. We had been so sure that we had found 'the one', and it had been so easy. In fact, if truth be known, we had almost been smug about this: we could not see what all the big fuss was about – you just have to be yourself and someone will come along, and you will just know they are the one for you, and it will all work out. But it didn't work out. We had had the dream, and then we had lost it, just like that. It was not so easy after all.

And so apart from feeling distraught, we also felt a little bit stupid and terribly confused. Nothing made sense anymore. Apart from the loss of pride among family and peers, we were now being followed around by, 'I told you so,' and, 'There's plenty more fish in the sea.' How could we have suddenly lost those feelings that just days before seemed so undeniably sublime and true? What was the point of it all? Why had we wasted our time, only to be hurt and disappointed? Where would we go from here? Was love really worth it? We told ourselves that it just was not worth it, and we would never do it again.

And yet in no time at all, like an alcoholic who falls off the wagon, we resumed our deluded quest to find the ideal mate: brainwashing is tough to shake.

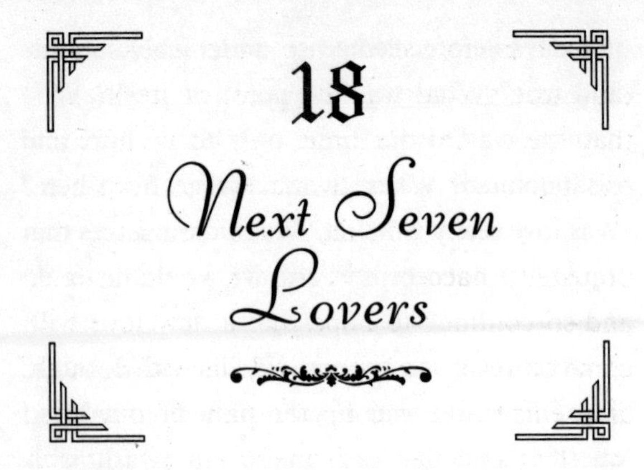

18 Next Seven Lovers

Although we have been badly stung, burnt and afflicted, we are straight back out there on the razzle in search of a replacement. Other than the indoctrination we were subjected to as children, there are two other reasons why we resume our search for 'the one' after the collapse of our first love.

First, we believe that the only way we will get over the pain of losing love is by finding another to love.

Second, we want our first love to see us with someone else before we see them with some other fucker, thereby inflicting more pain on them, and hopefully diminishing some of our own, by transferring it onto them also.

Neither provides us with much comfort. It is only time, and an acceptance of the inevitable – that love cannot last forever – which will in the end help us overcome the heartache.

And yet it seems that many of us are not prepared to accept this truth for a long time, and so continue to hope that a new love will come our way and will provide us with enough amusement to cover up the pain of our loss. We struggle to recognize that it is always our First Love we are trying to get over, and yet the reason why this love *was* so astonishing is because it was the first, because we knew nothing better, which made it innocent and perfect. We seriously thought that we had found our destiny, our life partner, our 'one and only', but this was not to be, and so we have to make up for lost time and lost love by gaining as much experience as possible, with as many people as possible in as short a time as possible!

Lover One we take on the re-bound, very soon after we have lost our First Love, and this is doomed from the start because our heart and soul are not in the mood for love. Hence, it is nothing more than a brief fling, with little or no substance, and in no time at all time catches up with us once again. Failed.

There are, of course, some complete and utter idiots who marry on the rebound, and such people do nothing more than prove my basic thesis about why people marry.

Lover Two we take when we are coming down to earth a little more, when we have come to realize that the whole love game is not as easy as we first thought. We give a little less of ourselves while at the same time giving our new lover more leeway with their funny little ways. They are unfaithful because we are too damn 'nice'. We find out, feel hurt and angry, then walk away. Failed.

Lover Three is when we get tough: we are not going to be betrayed again. And so we do not do what we say we are going to do, we are always late, and we show little or no respect. In short, we take out all our anger – built up from the three previous failures – on this person. Our actions are utterly irrational and unfair, but we commit them all the same. In fact, we behave so badly that he or she finally dumps us because we are 'a shit'. Failed.

Lover Four is a foregone conclusion: as soon as we have spent one day with this person, we are sure it is going to fail. Again, we make no effort – we are still feeling rather sorry for ourselves – and figure, 'What's the point anyway?' It does not take long for him or her to become profoundly aggravated by our ambivalence. The relationship ends as fast as it begun – no surprise there – in fact, we are quite glad. Failed.

Lover Five is when it dawns on us that if we are ever going to be happy in a relationship, we must make a far greater effort with our lovers. We need to remember who we really are and we need to start being that person, not some idiot we have never met. This means being fair, considerate, enthusiastic and giving. Hence, Lover Five gets a good go at us: we are finally happier in ourselves, and so are prepared to show him or her who we genuinely are. However, though we enjoy our time with this person, they are not truly our type, and we suddenly realize that all our nice and decent behaviour is to our detriment: it is not leading us to where we want to be, with the person we want to be with (remember, we are still – at this stage in our romantic development – in pursuit of 'the one'). With this new awareness, we are faced with a choice. Either we call up the person, arrange to meet, confess it is not working for us anymore, and hurt them; or we do not call, and avoid picking up the phone altogether… in fact, we go completely AWOL… and when he or she at long last does manage to get hold of us, we deliver such a poor and feeble explanation that they no longer trust or understand us and it is over. The second choice always wins. Failed.

Lover Six heralds a more pragmatic outlook: we have accepted that although everyone is different, there is always something we can find in common with someone we desire, and if, in the unlikely event, there is nothing… well, then we can always pretend to share an interest with this person on some subject or another in order to get them into bed. You see, we have become so cynical by now that we will do anything just to take another lover for a while, and to this end we are prepared to compromise, even alter, our entire personality. And yet, aside from the sex, we are unhappy from the start and resent everything this lover says, even if it is something as trivial as, 'Good morning'. We instantly start thinking, 'Is it? Is it a good morning? No it isn't because I'm with you.' Of course this is doomed to fail, and does.

Lover Seven. Well, here we are – our First Love and six lovers down the line – cynical and single. We have decided that lovers are more hassle than they are worth and we are no longer in need or want of them: prostitution is about to become a more viable and honest alternative! But then the inevitable happens. We are out one night with friends and we meet someone who we really click with, feel comfortable around and who makes us feel good about ourselves. We talk to this person the next day, twice in fact – something we normally don't do because we are, by now, so used to playing games at the start of a relationship – then we meet up that same night, and well… boom, boom, boom… we might as well have died and gone to heaven. Yesss!

19 First Big Relationship

Oh my God, this is amazing, it's unbelievable… we have found our soulmate; life really is worth living, love really is worth waiting for.

Every minute of every day is divided into ecstasy or agony. We feel ecstatic when we are with First Big Relationship (FBR) person, and in agony when we are apart. It is so much better than (our) First Love, because we have now lived more, and have discovered how hard it is to find someone we really, truly, madly, deeply love. We even say things like, 'I *thought* I was in love before, but that was not love compared to how I feel now.' (Idiot!)

And yet the principal reason why we feel so marvellous is that our desperate yearning has at last been fulfilled: we have reaped what we believe we deserved after all the disappointments we have been through, the long line of failed love affairs. At last we have found out what our parents meant when they said, 'You get what you deserve if you work hard enough for it,' and the saying 'practice makes perfect' makes sense.

And so in the months that follow life takes a turn for the better, we go for lavish dinners we cannot justify, spend consecutive weekends in a hotel and buy our FBR expensive gifts which we cannot afford and they don't deserve, but that's okay – this is *real* love.

Even our phone bill goes through the roof; all of our work colleagues know everything about FBR though they have not yet met him or her; and our boss gets more and more irritated at all the personal phone calls we are suddenly receiving (but we don't care). At the same time, our friends sigh with boredom as we recount 'just one more thing' about FBR – we are incapable of talking about anyone or anything else – but we continue to ramble on incessantly about our amazing new life, despite their obvious lack of interest.

After a short while, the subject of living together arises. And we and our FBR decide that because we spend so much time with one another, we might as well live together. Yes, we can pool our resources and create a better lifestyle. And so we do just this, move in together, and this action takes us one (fatal) step closer to matrimony.

And yet time slowly changes our attitude towards our FBR and we start to take things for granted: weekends away become a habit rather than an adventure, and instead of breakfast in bed, they are lucky to get a cup of coffee in the morning if they ask for it. All in all, familiarity breeds contempt, and the amazing and refreshing relationship we once had slowly transmutes into a *way of* living rather than a *reason for* living.

So once again, we are in a situation that we would rather not be in and are made to wonder what we should do. Perhaps we ought to give up because the relationship has now become mundane, driven by arguments about toothpaste and toilet seats? We speculate about how content our friends are with their partners, wonder whether we would be happier if we were single again, and yet at the same time fear how we would cope without our FBR?

Or there again, maybe we should just value what we have and strive for the end goal of marriage (according to our narrow worldview, time is running out for us and we must settle down soon, or else). To this extent, we must raise our doubts with our FBR, express them, work through them, compromise, and then make a lasting commitment. And so we are faced with a choice: leave or stay.

Okay, let us explore the latter first of all. We decide to stay because we believe that only by working hard at a relationship will it result in a happy and abiding conclusion, namely marriage: we convince ourselves (silently) that we might be unhappy at the moment but things will change once we are married; 'M' will enliven the relationship, make us passionate once more. However, this is a cop out, a cheap but emotionally and financially expensive trick which tucks us away in a temporary 'safety zone'. The 'stay to get married' option is merely a way to inject some excitement into the relationship. It is a way of avoiding the real issues by offering another adventure for us to concentrate on – to distract us. Such diligence is self-deceptive and feeble: we want to be married simply because we cannot face being alone, and in this respect 'M' provides nothing more than an emotional crutch. Once a relationship has reached this point, failure is, without fail, the ultimate conclusion.

Now let us look at the former option. Leave. This is the harder of the two options, because, although the relationship is now mundane and we cannot go on flogging a dead horse, we are going to hurt someone we really love. And so we tell FBR as truthfully and as gently as possible that it is time to end the charade, and it is time for us to leave (well done, that was very brave!), and we agree to remain friends (heard that one before). We then call every day (for a week or two), not only to ensure that he or she is okay but also to alleviate our guilt. Again time passes, the pain and sense of loss diminishes, and then we resume our search once more.

There are those of us who will simply go through another Next Seven Lovers and come to the same crossroads five years later: should we stay or should we go? But this time, we stay, because time really is ticking by and unless we settle down right now, then perhaps we never will, (now wouldn't that be terrible?) and so we pop the question... and well, that is it (marriage, children, boredom, divorce – same old story!)

Or there are those of us who do not go through another seven lovers but rather become lonely and depressed not long after we have left our FBR, and so begin to wonder whether he or she was 'the one' after all: we continue to call out of duty, need and loneliness, but our heart has been weakened beyond repair, and we cannot bear the thought of starting all over again, so we crack under the pressure – this is driven less by him or her than by our own frailty – we simply need someone else in our life. And so we run back into the arms of FBR for security and comfort with our tail between our legs, like some prodigal lover, full of clichés about how we nearly lost our soulmate, our one and only (apart from the ones before), our one great love, our... just wake me up when I've finished.

20 Weddings

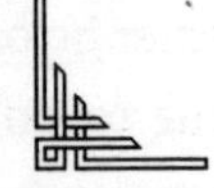

We finally come to the part where marriage is inevitable, where the excuses have run out and the wedding has to be planned and executed. (Note the use of the word 'executed'.)

Allow me to cut to the chase and tell you the truth about weddings. In short, they are a twenty-four-hour-a-day 'anxiety attack'. Ask anyone who has had the misfortune to have one and they will *all* tell you the same thing – the months leading up to the 'Big Day' were fraught with stress and complication. And if they say otherwise, they are a liar, or they have selective Alzheimer's. I mean, come on. There is the incessant organization – which church, food and music. The politics – he wants one thing, she wants another, and the outlaws (who are paying) want something else. The time-consuming costume fittings for an outfit that will be worn once – it's almost immoral. And then, after all this obsessive and indulgent preparation, the Big Day, when it finally comes, be it in a French chateau or a Sidcup registry office, is unoriginal and lacklustre, a parody of itself. Trying to please everyone never works. Weddings try to please everyone.

But this is not how the bride and groom see it, no. Their love is on show and it is unique and spectacular. Their Big Day – the culmination of years of frantic searching, expectation, bad dates and drunken one-night stands – is their moment of glory, their chance to be the centre of attention, and they will make the very most of it. And so they are afflicted by delusions of grandeur... no, more than this, by a kind of 'marital monomania'. Yes, their wedding will be the wedding to end all weddings! It might be just another bloody wedding to everybody else – a day which will be forgotten in no time at all (probably by the next wedding, the following weekend) – but it is not this to them, the 'happy couple'. No, they are determined for this day to be glorified and etched in their minds for as long as they both shall live and for as long as their unsuspecting children can endure.

If we stand back, just for a moment, and look at weddings from a distance… well, they are clearly very strange affairs indeed, their components resembling more the idiosyncratic rituals of some dubious cult with an irrational ideology than traditional practices designed to mark and celebrate the beginning of the social and legal interdependence of two people.

First, there is the bride and her army of bridesmaids – slaves for the day (as if the hen night wasn't bad enough) – who are forced to wear ugly dresses; of course these are cheap clones of the bride's, and are deliberately less flattering, because the bride chose them to make her bridesmaids look less beautiful. They are then obliged to buy expensive wedding gifts from a bland, regimented, overpriced and unromantic wedding list that does nothing more than insult their sensibilities. And, as if this isn't enough, they then have to deal with the bride herself – the princess – who has been afflicted by a kind of noxious egotism since becoming the centre of attention, and is consequently almost intolerable to be around: she has convinced herself that she is special because she is getting married. And although she thinks that all her friends want to be a part of her wedding, in actuality they do not. For most of them, it is an expense that they can ill afford, and one that makes them ill to have to afford. But they go through with it nevertheless, though end up regretting their involvement all the same. (As they say, 'No good deed goes unpunished.')

For the groom it is a different story – his stag night is his last chance to 'get laid' before it becomes adultery. Or it is the time when he is humiliated by his friends in order to stay 'one of the boys'. Whichever it is, after this last-ditch dive into freedom, the groom is stepping into the great abyss that is married life. He has to endure all of his bride's drama before, during and after the wedding; and then they each have to endure each other's relatives for the wedding, and beyond. And as for his ushers, they are obliged to organize his gallant send off in as debauched a way as possible, and yet have to maintain an air of sanctity when it comes to the actual ceremony, and must never speak of the groom's dirty little secrets for the duration of the marriage. (As they say, 'No good deed...')

Weddings are nothing more than a compromise for the groom and a fairytale for the bride. Enough is enough. They are characterized by hideous expense (all that money can surely be put to better use), obscene self-glorification, cheesy music, pink-and-white tablecloths, an over-abundance of mixed flower arrangements, appalling teenage 'summer job' waiters, and not very good food. To my female reader, let me say that dressing up like a meringue is hardly representative of genuine love and future happiness. And to my male reader, let me say that looking like a funeral director with a snazzy waistcoat points to something sinister and macabre rather than something noble and benevolent. Let me also stress that there is nothing pleasurable either in watching awkward and overweight men stumble through unamusing speeches or in listening to people around us waffle on about 'What a lovely couple the bride and groom make!' or 'How beautiful the bride looks!' I mean, let's be honest, these fellow guests are hardly going to say the opposite – that the couple look bored with one another already, that the groom will most likely be fucking someone else within six months, and that beneath that dress and all that make up, the bride is a bit of an old dog – unless, of course, they are prepared to be ostracized for the remainder of the evening, and marriage. (That would be about two years, then.)

I am sorry to go on about this, but I feel I must. It is simply beyond me how two people and their respective families are prepared to turn a *single* Saturday afternoon into one of the greatest expenses of their lives: Christ, some of them even go so far as to re-mortgage their houses in order to pay for the Big Day that everyone else forgets! And so it becomes an obsession, it consumes the collective consciousness of both families, and they can talk and think of nothing else. They are, of course, amazed at the difficulties they encounter along the way in trying to implement their pathetic and forgettable plans, which would not exist if they hadn't created them; but they blunder their way through the drama, as if it is some kind of important world event. Please, I would like to know, what the fuck did they talk about before they planned a wedding?

My relatives used to come up to me at weddings, poke me playfully in the ribs, and say, 'You're next!' They stopped doing this, however, after I did the same to them at funerals.

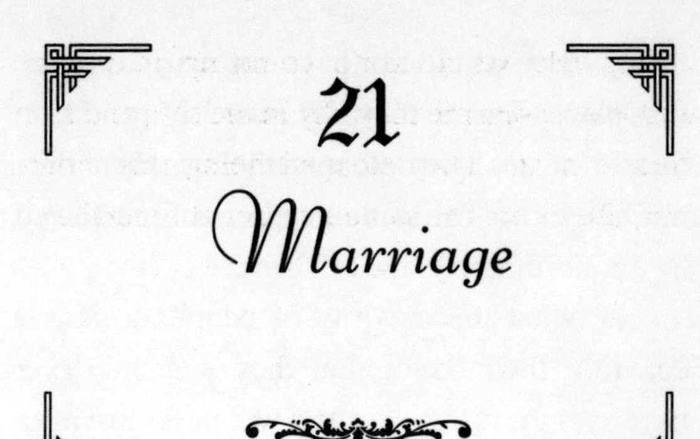

21 Marriage

And so the big day comes and the big day goes... whether it went well or not is unimportant since it will all be reduced to a dinner-party anecdote in no time at all. And thus now it is all about the marriage itself.

Let me say right away that the majority of married people are straight up fucking liars. I mean... come on, do they honestly believe that they are absolutely committed to the contractual obligations of the union they have entered into, that they *have* never or *will* never kiss, caress or fuck somebody else? Surely if they had really considered these obligations prior to getting married – because they wanted to determine whether or not they could realistically honour them – they would not have got married in the first place. And if they did seriously reflect on them but got married nonetheless, then they must be either deluded or repressed or afflicted by an inordinately low sex drive.

No, what the majority of people do is just convince their fiancé that they will only ever have eyes for him or her and will never lust after anyone else; and though the fiancé knows, deep down, that this conviction goes against the very grain of human desire and experience, he or she chooses to believe it all the same.

To address those stubborn masses who *still* refuse to acknowledge the warning signs, who *still* think that things will be different for you, and who *still* believe that marriage offers greater happiness, despite all that I have written to the contrary thus far, I suppose I have to admire your unwavering faith in human nature, your utter lack of grip on reality. However, I ask you to consider this: why, if you love someone, is it necessary to marry them? Surely your love will survive without marriage, won't it? Or is marriage the only thing that can hold you together because there is doubt? You see, marriage is built on insecurity, the insecurity that needs *proof.* If proof is needed, then there is doubt. If there is doubt, then marriage by its very nature is built on weak and shaky foundations. And if you do not need proof, then why do you need marriage? There is no trust, love and belief in marriage – if there was there would be no need for marriage in the first place.

Here is a statistic: seventy percent of divorcees knew that their marriage was going to fail, even as they walked down the aisle. Now there's a statistic I like!

And here is an observation: there is a common thread that runs through the reasoning behind a woman's need to marry, and on the many occasions when I have mentioned that I do not believe in marriage, women, more often than not, explode, 'But what about children? There is no way that I am going to have a baby with someone unless we are married! No way! If I am having a baby with someone he's going to be held responsible if he wants to leave me!' What?! My God, if this is your main argument for marriage, then please do not get married. Or breed.

So, ... back to our young newlyweds ... Assuming they make it through the first few months, or if they are lucky, first few years of marital bliss, the time will surely come when 'the itch' sets in.

When they were first married, it was wonderful: they were made to feel important, not least because every time they mentioned they were just married, people would invariably respond with smiles and congratulations, but also because they were welcomed into 'established society' – they were married now like all good, decent people... and would have children soon like all good, decent people. But as time went by, the two of them felt less special and less privileged, and began to question what their decision to marry had actually done for them, for their relationship. In reality, it had not made it any better, any more solid or any more fun. Rather it was still plagued by the same irritations, the same differences, the same reluctant compromises.

And so when 'the itch' finally needs to be relieved, each of them is faced with a great dilemma: flout the rules of the contract and find relief on the side, or admit defeat and leave the marriage. There are some who are so reluctant to endure the pain, humiliation and expense of divorce that they elect for the former, whereas there are others who simply give up and walk away, perhaps finally realizing that marriage is a flawed construct.

This latter group, although a bunch of failures, should not feel guilty – people change in different ways and at different times (it is often the thing which most attracted us to someone that we end up finding the least attractive thing about him or her just years later) – in fact, such change is inevitable. Sadly, marriage does not allow for this most fundamental aspect of human existence.

We tend to love things that are new, attractive and engrossing, but once in our possession, if we cannot fully control them we quickly become frustrated, and this annoyance can easily become hatred. We might find someone's individuality irresistible at first – 'She's so unique!' we swoon – but as time passes, we come to resent this person for not being like us, or like we want her to be, and so seek to change her. The person we thought we loved becomes increasingly distant, until we end up leading an almost completely separate life from her, despite still living under the same roof. Basically we are left trying to salvage a lost cause, arguing about nothing in particular and caring about nothing at all.

This all sounds very depressing, because it is. Nobody wants to live unhappily, nobody wants perpetual aggravation as a daily routine, nobody wants to be seen as a failure; but marriages do fail. They do not always end in divorce, and they are not unhappy all of the time, but they are, more often than not, a real struggle; an emotional and practical failure.

If there are children involved, then there might be good reason to stick it out a few more years (at least until they are a little older), but if not, then the only sensible thing to do is to get out while there is still a chance to forge a new life, and find a new love.

Nearly sixty percent of all marriages end in divorce, and of the forty percent that survive, only two or three percent proceed amicably to their conclusion, until one party dies. Thus, the remainder are just miserable failures. Allow me to offer up an analogy: if marriage is a leap of faith, let us assume that we are in an aeroplane waiting to parachute to the ground. Just before we leap, we are given the following statistics: there is a sixty percent chance that you will die and a forty percent chance that you will survive. Now the question is: do you still jump? If you do (because you are insane or suicidal), allow me to clarify. Of the forty percent likelihood that you survive, there is a ninety percent likelihood that you will break a bone, some ribs, your pelvis or suffer permanent brain damage. Now, do you still want to jump knowing that there is only a two or three percent possibility that you will walk away with only a sprained ankle? Hardly good odds, and yet this is the leap of faith that marriage offers.

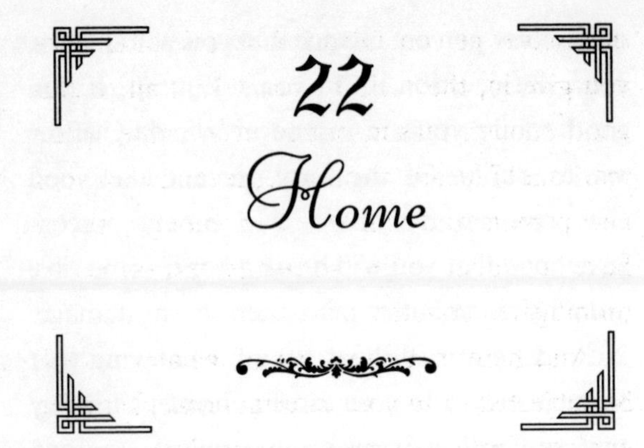

22 Home

Married, hitched, whatever, you are now in the 'enviable' position of being expected to invite the *whole* family to your new marital home, in-laws and outlaws included.

The reason for this sudden change of fortune is that the majority of your family simply did not want to visit you when you were living together in a state of sin. But now, now that you are married (you have God's blessing after all)...well, it is more acceptable for the older generations to finally see you sharing the same bedroom, bathroom and wardrobes. Believe me, you *will* be a host in your new home. In fact, you will now find that you literally cannot keep the guests away: they are bloody throwing themselves at you for an invitation, and once you give in, they will be back. Isn't all of this good enough reason not to even contemplate marriage? I mean, come on... dealing with your *own* parents and family is bad enough, but to have to deal with someone else's is an unmitigated disaster.

And here is a short list of what you will be subjected to in your marital home: showing endless family members around the house which you just cleaned in time for their arrival; praying that you don't burn the Sunday roast; dreading the trauma of hosting a family Christmas; boasting about your garden (yawn); feigning interest in yet another 'first marital home' anecdote recounted by one of your in-laws; enduring gossip about some couple you have never heard of, will probably never meet and, quite frankly, do not want to meet; and pretending to have a great time with a bunch of incontinent old fogies, who once and for all dispel the popular notion that wisdom comes with age.

Oh my God, this is frightening. In fact, I must confess that just writing about this is now making me feel anxious. I'm suddenly struggling to breathe. What is happening to me? This is a nightmare that will never go away. In fact it's worse than a nightmare, it is cold, stark naked, bone-crunching reality... it's fucking real. And as far as I can see it will never stop.

Marriage is a threateningly dull and mundane reality, you see. It has to be, because if you are too concerned with your own happiness and fulfilment, then consequently you are not giving enough attention to your partner, and you are not concentrating sufficiently on the marriage or on building a home... and well, that is just not good enough. To have a successful marriage, you are forced to be conservative, sensible, perhaps even boring. This would at least account for the 'white picket fence phenomenon' the world is afflicted by, each marital home on the street, and in the neighbourhood, determined to portray itself as more wealthy, more happy and more complete than the one next door.

Let us be honest here, marriage hardly inspires progressive and adventurous behaviour (affairs excluded). No, it requires sacrifice, lots of it, too much to mention... in fact, too much to make it reasonable, let alone feasible. I, for one, am not up for it; nor for the in-laws. Thanks, but no thanks.

The marital home of your dreams can stay right there – in your dreams . . . the 'realital' home is nothing but a living nightmare.

23 Sex and Marriage

Well, this is a bit like a steam train that runs out of coal and comes to a slow, grinding halt. However, unlike a fuel-less train, it does not stop completely, but rather becomes so infrequent and unmemorable that it ends up being too embarrassing to speak of.

There is only one way to keep sex going during marriage – have an affair.

If you want to remain sexually active without committing adultery – do not get married.

24 Marriage and Children

There are many reasons for having children: we love them and want to be a great parent; we fancy yet more possessions; we are determined to leave a legacy; we are bored in our marriage and feel unloved; we simply cannot think of any other way to hold on to our husband or wife.

Now it should be pretty obvious, I hope, which one of the above is a good motive, but in case you are in any doubt, it is the first, and only the first reason: the others are nothing more than pathetic and unacceptable.

And yet, the decision to have a child is both intricate and complex, or at least it should be. There are fundamental questions we ought to ask ourselves before having a child: do we really yearn to be a full-time parent? Are we genuinely patient? Do we have the necessary time to dedicate to a child? Are we in a financial position to support and sustain a child, or are we going to resent our child for providing us with endless financial worry? Will we be able to alleviate any suffering our child might go through? Are we going to end up providing our child with a split home and endless confusion? Is our home a squat? Is our bank a tin box? Is our CV a criminal record? Have we ever been in a mental hospital for the criminally insane?

All of these might seem like fairly obvious questions which require brute honesty to answer, and yet the majority of us when answering them are not entirely honest: we either lack self-awareness, or are just 'economical' with the truth.

We all know married people who, even though they are perpetually busy and work-obsessed, displaying irascibility more often than calm, egotism more often than selflessness, nevertheless still feel it is their right and duty, as a married member of society, to have children; and we are immediately made to wonder what on earth it must be like for their offspring, who are bred with a huge disadvantage, because to them this is 'normal'. Such married people would be good candidates for a sterilization operation, because when they have a child, they only serve to make things worse for everyone, including themselves.

Then there are those married couples we know who have children in order to fill some dreadful gap in their lives: to take away the pain of a loveless and directionless marriage. They think they will at least find happiness through parenthood; this will be their *raison d'être*, because they have no other idea how they should occupy their pitiful existence. This is just plain selfish, and only serves to produce yet more screwed up children.

All children need love and consistency. These are the two main ingredients for turning a child into a happy and well-adjusted adult. (This is not just my opinion, it is a fact.) They also need structure and discipline. And marriage, as you can see by the epidemic rate of divorce, does not provide any of these essential ingredients for a young and impressionable child.

And so let me assert right now that it is not necessary to be married in order to have a child.

Surely it is preferable to be a single parent who displays constant love and affection for their child, rather than a married parent who either resents the child for adversely affecting the marriage or ignores the child in order to argue with their spouse.

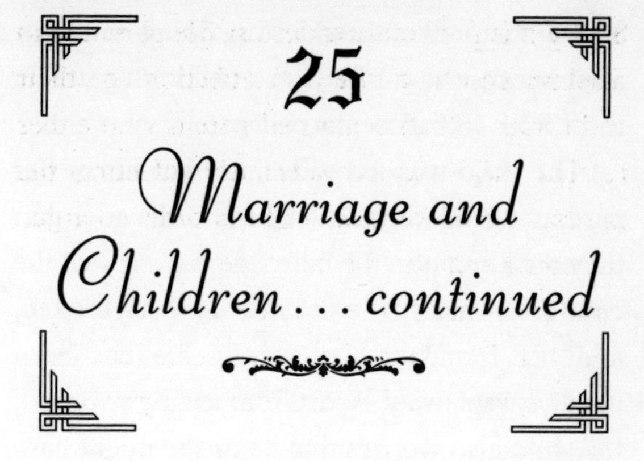

25

Marriage and Children . . . continued

Allow me to continue with this idea of having children outside marriage. It does not follow that a child born outside the institution will necessarily be more deprived and insecure than if he or she was born within it: we only have to look at the current divorce rate to comprehend that the precious model of marriage and children, 'the good and wholesome family life' is being ruined and rejected at an epidemic rate.

The needs of a child are not met by the institution of marriage itself, but rather by the child's parents – what they actually do to love and nurture their child. Currently, the majority of us still continue to put immense faith in a structure that is proving to be increasingly flimsy and archaic. We should stop doing this, not least because it is *always* the child who suffers most from its failure, its collapse.

The child was led to believe that his or her parents would be married *forever*, but now that they are apart and the marriage is over, well the child feels cheated – a promise has been broken, and the foundation of family life has been cruelly swept away. Apart from feeling wronged, the child also worries that he or she might have been partly responsible for the collapse of their family life, and so is riddled with complex feelings of guilt, sadness, remorse and shame. Alongside this, the child now has to deal with a whole new situation, new homes, new school and even new parents. And yet, had the child's parents not married, had they presented him or her with another worldview (that people need not marry in order to have children, that romantic love does not last forever, and that their child was born into a loving and responsible relationship), then the child would not be so lost and distraught now: no promise would have been broken.

But do we *really* need to get hitched to have children? This is, of course, the reason that many people give for getting married – 'Well, it's because we want to have kids' – and this sentiment, more than any other, I have utter contempt for. That more than half of marriages end in divorce while the remainder consist of incessant argument, boredom and dissatisfaction – the children left to wonder why on earth their parents married in the first place – should be reason enough not to marry.

The common, dysfunctional, marital unit: Mum (who resents her husband's absence and existence) dealing with the children during the week, trying to maintain some semblance of discipline; and Dad seeing them so rarely (because he works all week and has too much to do at the weekends) that he ends up spoiling them to curry favour, thereby undoing all of Mum's hard work. This picture causes one to question why on earth marriage is perceived to be a good breeding ground?

I want to banish the idea that being married makes you a better parent: this is a formulation cooked up by the moral majority. There are many people who cannot conceive a world of their own, who are unable to give their own life meaning, and thus tell us that we can *only* lead a 'good and meaningful life' if we follow the line and example set by them, the majority: this is the logic of consensus. Surely a child about to be born into this world would do better to have an unmarried parent who has thoroughly considered the responsibility of parenthood, appreciates its magnitude and yet is nevertheless willing to be an attentive parent, rather than a married parent who has walked blindly down the aisle and sees the child-to-be merely as an inevitable consequence of marriage and an extension of his or her withering ego.

Next on the list of reasons why unmarried parents might be more desirable for a child is that they are more likely to remain better friends for a longer period: that they are not married should afford them the necessary space in their relationship, particularly if each of them maintains their own individual home, and in this way the child spends quality time with *each* parent.

And if they do decide to go their own separate ways and pursue new romantic relationships, this will be seen as something that was always a possibility, and therefore they will not then be consumed by a lengthy and acrimonious divorce, in which the child's future is ultimately decided in a court of law. You see, that the child has parents who considered the choice to have a child *more* important than the choice to marry puts him or her in a far better position when the parents negotiate their own separate lives: the child, not the marriage, has always been their focus, and he or she will continue to be just this.

Children do not care about marriage, society does.

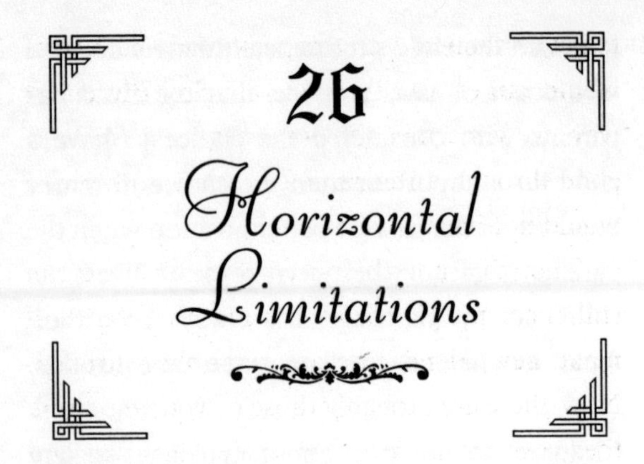

26 Horizontal Limitations

It is clear that when we marry we limit our horizons, restrict our freedom and contradict our nature. Before we are married, before we live with someone, we can do what we want, when we want. We thrive off this freedom: we never know who we are going to meet or where we are going to meet them, and of the people we do meet, there are always those who enchant us, impress us, stimulate us or affect us. We are aware that every person we encounter holds countless possibilities, and we are free to explore these hopes, these prospects. We can spend as much or as little time as we like with a particular person, can make last minute plans with him or her, and can decide whether we want to get horizontal with this person or whether we would rather wait for someone else. But either way, we have met someone new and we have gone through an experience that we otherwise would not have gone through.

Though I am obviously aware that we can still meet people if we are married, can still make new friends, we are certainly restricted. Now, there are probably those of you who think that your marriage will be different – you and your spouse will grant one another great freedom – but let me assure you that once you are married, the institution will reveal itself as illiberal, authoritarian and oppressive: this is its fundamental nature. It has firm rules and regulations that must be observed in order to maintain its success.

Thus, once married, if we meet someone we like and we want to spend time with this person, it is important that our spouse likes him or her as well. And if our spouse does not, then we are faced with a choice: either sacrifice a potentially important and fulfilling friendship or face a barrage of criticism and suspicion from our spouse.

Then on top of this, even if we do boldly opt for the latter, our relationship with this person will always be limited by virtue of the fact that we are married. Our status as a married person becomes an invisible barrier to the friendship: it impedes it, restricts it. And so when we see the friend, we must never spend too long with him or her, and if our spouse accompanies us, well then the friend must be kept firmly at arm's length. We also find that we cannot be utterly honest with our friend (as we would be if alone) when our spouse is with us: we can hardly confess how attracted we are to the person on the next table! In fact, our spouse must be constantly reassured that he or she is more important than the friend, and always will be. And if there happens to be a disagreement between our spouse and our friend, well then, the onus is firmly on us to side with our spouse, however bloody unreasonable he or she is being.

And so, although marriage seems to provide a certain 'security', what invariably happens is that this security becomes a limitation that curtails our ability to experience new people; and although we have made a vow to 'build a life' with just one person, our natural instinct tells us otherwise, and so the security that marriage provides suddenly becomes a box, which we can only escape temporarily, and must always climb back into at the end of every day. And so, frustrated, we seek out others. We once again want to embrace the unknown, the unexpected. It is surely this need which drives people to have affairs – we always want to do what we are not allowed to!

The single life might be perceived as less stable, but it is a lot less stale.

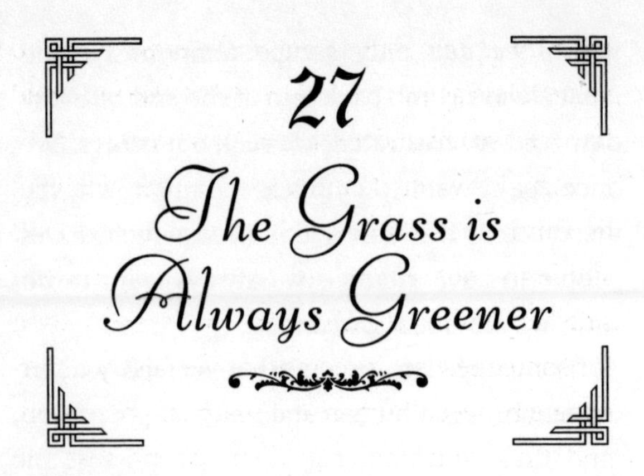

27 The Grass is Always Greener

All of us are afflicted by the thought that things might be better if we had *this* instead of *that*: in fact, it is this perpetual state of restlessness and dissatisfaction that controls most humans.

Consumer society has flourished for this very reason: it panders to this most fundamental aspect of human nature, offering us things which are supposedly better than the things we already have, to the extent that even if what we presently have fulfils us, we are nevertheless driven to buy and consume the next thing put before us, because it might bring us *even more* happiness, *even more* fulfilment. We are always wanting, always looking for something more, something different. We might value what we have for a time, but sooner or later we come to value it less as we conceive of what else we could have, as we fall under the spell of something new.

And yet when it comes to marriage, we seem to think that this aspect of our nature will suddenly not apply: no, we will be forever satisfied with one person and will never yearn for someone else. It seems that we falsely differentiate between human and material possession, and thus conclude that when we possess the former, we will not suffer from restlessness. This logic is flawed, not least because we cannot even endure a car or a stereo for more than a few years, and a human being is far more temperamental and volatile than a car or a stereo.

Unbelievably, when we do become unhappy and unsettled, or our spouse does, we are suddenly overtaken by surprise, disbelief and heartache, and wonder why we were unable to find lifelong contentment with this one person.

Christ, all we had to do was confront reality in the first place! I have little (or no) sympathy for those who weep and whine when all they need do is accept certain inherent and all too obvious aspects of their humanity.

We are gluttons – let's face the truth about this – we are never happy with what we have for long, always seeking the next best thing. Why deny this natural instinct in us? It is natural for us to want to move on, *un*natural for us to be static. Marriage tries to stop the change, it is static, a false promise.

Let me ask, first, why it is that so many divorcees encourage their children to marry, and second, why it is that so many unhappy parents, who have endured a loveless marriage for more years than they care to remember, are so puzzled, upset and disappointed when their children complain of their own marriages, and subsequently get divorced? What the hell is going on here?! Why are we so determined to deceive, limit and stagnate ourselves? Why can't we embrace our need for change? Change is what sustains us.

Let's not be so 'green' about our desires and needs. It is only natural to value something for a while, and then to value change. Let's accept that we might want to look over the fence, and we might want to be there; other times we are happy where we are (and this is when we are in a great relationship). Let us accept that we will always want to keep expanding our realms of possibility.

28 Marriage and the Law

It would seem now that the laws surrounding marriage have become more important than the essence of the union. It seems that marriage has become a way for a woman to 'make sure' that she is not left in the lurch once she has had the baby, created the home, lost the art of seduction, and is overweight and unattractive. It would seem that men are made nervous by the enormity of the financial consequences of divorce.

Marriage no doubt used to favour the man. He could do what he wanted, when he wanted: he was master of the house, it was his money, he could take mistresses, and if he felt like it, he could divorce his wife and leave her penniless, broken and destitute, having shirked the responsibilities he was so keen to take on as a young man in order to fulfil his (or his parents') dreams. The law was firmly on his side, and he readily let himself be corrupted by this male-oriented institution.

However, now it seems that the law favours the woman: in fact, so much so that some women are now driven to marry in order to avoid another mundane job, to be kept by a husband, to raise children, and to leave the worrying to someone else. Many women 'con' men into marriage in order to ensure a secure future for themselves – with or without him – and to validate their existence as someone who is worth marrying. Often the divorce settlement is the only security a marriage offers.

Marriage is a law unto itself. The bitter consequences of marriage are a disaster that fill our courts daily, and so fill the pockets of our lawyers fully: marital law is big business, and has nothing to do with love, trust, belief or commitment. In fact, these laws negate every single good thing in any relationship. There is a certain irony here: it costs little or nothing in legal fees to marry, but it costs everything to divorce.

We must wonder why marriage need be a legal contract. Perhaps because marriage was designed to protect the untrusting and the insecure: the stamp of the law gives these people the requisite sense of trust and security; it encourages the weak to take the plunge; it is a cage that holds two untrusting people side by side. Very often, the law of marriage (with the price of divorce) is the only thing that keeps two people together. The law is their 'commitment'. And so this is a 'leap of doubt' rather than one of faith, and the certainty it provides is typically short-lived. The law of marriage proves itself to be a man-made, artificial institution that cannot even stand up to its own rules.

Then there is the question of why society pushes us to marry, and why the law favours the married over the unmarried: the former are not only granted tax breaks, but other favourable benefits as well. Why would the government encourage a woman to give up her freedom in order to be controlled by a man? And why would the government encourage a man to give up his freedom in order to be responsible for a wife? It seems that our governments are determined to pair us all off, with no regard for the fact that it is detrimental to our long-term financial health! And even these over-promoted 'financial benefits' of marriage are wiped out and negated by the 'financial catastrophe' of a divorce – this applies to and affects both men and women.

And yet these very same governments show rather less enthusiasm when it comes to gay marriage. Homosexuals, despite their success at maintaining relationships without 'the institution', now aspire to marry as well; such is the allure of state benefits and the pressure of conformity: their sexuality might have set them apart, but marriage will enable them to rejoin the consensus. And yet, the majority of governments (whether on religious, prejudicial, financial or legal grounds), still forbid gay couples to marry: they are in the minority after all, they are free thinkers, and they do not procreate, so why help them?

The law wears the guise of a helpful companion in times of trouble, a safety net when all else fails, when in reality (and like it or not, reality is where we live) it is there – in this sense at least – to confuse, complicate and contradict what it knows is the inevitable.

Is my argument beginning to make a little bit of sense?

29 Divorce

Guess what... it happens more often than not. It is the *one* thing that every married person thinks will happen to *somebody else*, and yet more often than not it comes sneaking round the corner and happens to *them*. And when it does, it is always, but always, a very difficult and painful affair: in fact so much so that we wonder how on earth anyone can bear to go through it... and yet millions do, every year.

These millions are driven to it because their marriage is so awful, is making them so unhappy, that even though they know how terrible a divorce can be, it is still the preferable option (imagine what marriage must be like).

And yet did they not agree to have and to hold, for better or for worse, for richer or for poorer, in sickness and in health, to love and to cherish, till death do they part? And so, by getting divorced, are they not breaking these vows they made, are they not conceding failure? Yes, they are!

And yet, their lapse, their defeat is hardly surprising, and the only thing they can really be held to account for is their failure to really consider what they were committing themselves to when they said, 'I do.'

Some will insist in their defence that they did just this – thoroughly contemplated marriage before embarking on it – and yet the person they married changed and became someone they no longer knew. Well, there's a bloody surprise! We all change, all the time, and so to expect the person they marry to stay the same is more stupid than…well, than setting alight Christmas pudding.

Are you the same person, holding the same opinions and attitudes that you held ten years ago? I hope not, because if you are, then you are more boring than an oil drill, and nobody should want to marry you anyway.

I am fully aware that there are many, many people who consider marriage the very foundation of society, a virtuous and noble institution, without which we would all be utterly lost. These people want all of us to end up married; these people believe that a world without divorce is possible. What intolerable fools they are!

And then there are those who have been through a bitter divorce but are still determined to marry again: the second time, it will be different, they tell themselves; they will meet someone and be with them forever. Didn't they say exactly the same thing last time? Such wishful thinking is pure delusion!

You see, even those who *know* the truth cannot *tell* the truth. It seems that I am one of the few who want to spread the word: lawyers certainly won't tell you, because they would be poor if they did; doctors won't tell you, because there would be fewer arguments, fewer stressed out people, fewer babies born and less illness – therefore fewer patients and less money; priests won't tell you – fewer marriages, fewer divorces, fewer re-marriages, fewer christenings, no victims, no congregation; Mummy and Daddy won't tell you – no grandchildren, no legacy, no family name, no more; governments won't tell you, because two single people need two roofs instead of one – no space; and so the list goes on... along with the divorces.

If we do not marry, then we do not divorce. And prevention is always better than cure.

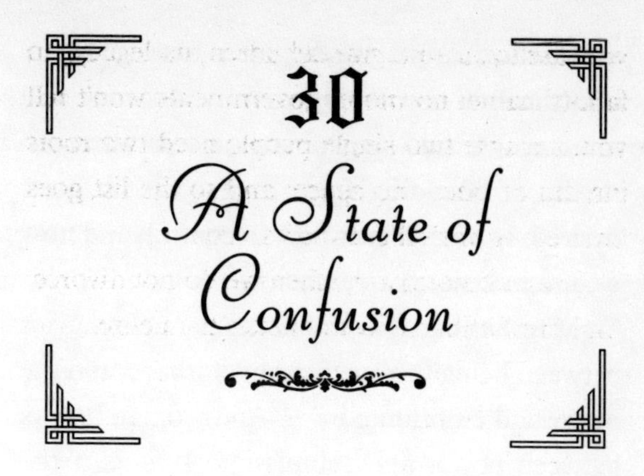

30 A State of Confusion

At present, we are living in a state of confusion, and men only have themselves to blame!

Because man has brute strength, he possessed woman. Fearful of the inner strength and ability of woman, he reduced her to 'housewife and mother' (don't get me wrong, I know this is not easy), and would not allow her to explore her true self. He made her dependant, and then he complained about it. Over the centuries woman was left with only one bargaining chip – sexual attraction, which she used in all its beguiling force to slowly place man in the weaker position.

Because man placed so much emphasis on his need for sex, and because woman was made to feel that she could not express herself sexually, a situation arose where man had to 'earn' sex (through courtship, chivalry, decency and marriage) from the woman he was attracted to. By withholding from man what he most desired, woman learnt how to control, and now we are in a state of confusion.

Man has become an anomaly – he struggles between being the overbearing husband and the newfound emotional lover. And woman hovers between power and submission. It is as if the submissive slave has begun to take control of the household and the master is finding it hard to adjust, as is the slave, who is not only asking questions, she is demanding answers.

We are dealing with a new society. A society that is slowly beginning to accept a woman's strength, finesse, loyalty and style; her ability to nurture and communicate. These attributes, so long ignored, place women on a level playing field, allowing them to assume control; and men are weakened – twice. Men are no longer the *possessors* of women, and they are fast becoming women's *possessions*.

And yet at the same time, it is not easy for modern women to shake off their legacy of inequality and oppression; it has been so indoctrinated into both men and women that marriage is some kind of necessary part of life that women are 'validated' by marriage – they are left to feel that unless married, their existence is somehow worthless. There are many girls who would rather be married and divorced than never married at all, because marriage is a sign that someone was prepared to make the commitment to them ('validated' their worth) even if it didn't work out.

And still, there are men who, if introduced to an attractive woman of thirty-five who has never been married, will ask, 'What's wrong with her?' – Christ! That's outrageous. Why doesn't he celebrate the chance to meet someone strong and independent?

Then, on the other hand, there are women who assume that an unmarried man of thirty-five is an 'eternal bachelor', as if this is a bad thing.

But this is where we are: in a world that values the ridiculous confines of the past, that does not celebrate the individual, and that scorns a woman who decides not to procreate.

Man is simply unable to accept the fact that, like him, woman not only *can*, but also *wants to*, have sex with more than one person, and that, like him, she need not love someone in order to have sex with them.

But what if men suddenly stopped wanting to possess women? Well then, the whole idea of 'infidelity' would be turned on its head. Imagine a world where men grant women sexual freedom, and vice versa. Would this not be a more loving world? For this proposed love would not constrain, but rather would grant the opposite: freedom.

We currently live in a world full of lies, where both men and women stray but insist to their spouses they do not (they are perfectly satisfied with one partner, they say). And yet, despite these assurances, neither sex trusts the other, and closely monitors the other's movements, even after they are married.

It is a funny thing, but if you allow your partner freedom of choice, then the chances are that they will still choose you, and if they don't, then they are not the right person for you to be with, at that time, anyway. It is often the case, ironically, that once we allow our partner to wander, to explore and to experiment they often no longer want or need to. For once we let them go they find that the thrill and the danger are diminished.

31 Marriage and Health

We often hear or read medical surveys which maintain that a good marriage is synonymous with good health, and a bad marriage with poor health. Well, how surprising! And what an utter waste of time and money. This does not boil down to the need for us to have a good marriage to be healthy; it boils down to … expectation.

You see, we are so indoctrinated that we need someone else to 'complete' us – that marriage is an essential part of life – that we end up with a neurosis that becomes the main reason for any date, love affair or relationship. We are led to believe that without marriage we have failed in one of our lifetime missions, that without marriage we are incomplete, and that without marriage we cannot be happy. And so, if we find a good partner, and we have a good marriage, we are happy, and therefore healthy.

On the other hand (the sixty percent and rising hard), if we happen to find someone who is 'good enough' (which is usually the case), and willing (which is usually the problem), there is a strong tendency to marry them because it is 'expected' of us and, unsurprisingly, we end up being unhappy. In this case, marriage becomes the scapegoat for our anger. Riddled with angst and confusion, doubt and fear, we are perpetually annoyed both with ourselves and with the world; we are frustrated, plagued by a sinking feeling whenever near our spouse; we are heavy-hearted, and – surprise, surprise – unhealthy.

Throughout our lives, we are sold this absurd formulation that marriage – pairing for life – is 'a natural state' that induces happiness and well-being (and that 'singledom' is a sickly state); but this is, put bluntly, utter bollocks! It might be a natural state for the traditional and the conservative, the stagnant and the boring among us – these people will say and do anything to defend their position – but it is not for anyone else. The expectation that someone else will complete us is our downfall: if we were not in such desperate need of someone else to provide us with peace of mind, I feel sure we would be much healthier.

And before we go any further, let me point out that no animal is set upon acquiring just *one* mate for life – wolves do not, ducks do not, and hippopotamuses do not... along with all the rest – and before any of you ask me to consider the male Black Widow spider: he *would* have more than one mate but for the fact that he is immediately killed and consumed by the female as soon as he has impregnated her.

Marriage and monogamy (or rather 'monotony') are not natural: by forcing ourselves into these two situations, we are simply trying to suppress what *is* natural; we are trying to control the uncontrollable, and we are failing miserably. A far more natural state is to be with someone while we are happy with them, and then to move on once we are no longer happy with them. Is it not better to accept and to embrace the inevitable changes that occur in our lives, and the lives of others, rather than to resist them with the inflexible construct of marriage?

On a final note regarding the single life, I am quite sure that the only thing making a single person sick is the thought of marriage, and if this decrepit institution were removed once and for all from our consciousness and put in its rightful place – on the scrap heap of society – then we would all be happy and we would all be healthy.

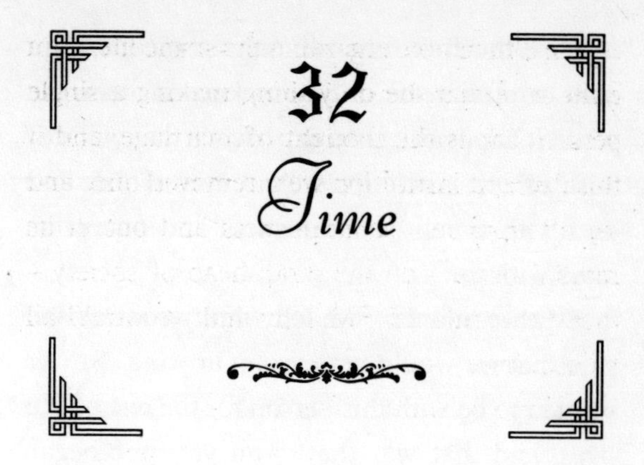

32 Time

Time is both the creator and the destroyer of relationships, and we have no control over it: it moves constantly, it is invisible and it is eternal. If every timepiece in the world were stopped, if every human being and every creature were killed, even if the whole world was destroyed... still the march of time would continue: it is all-powerful.

And yet there *are* occasions in our lives when time does appear to stop dead, be these the moments before a car crash, or other times when our life is in danger. And there is one other time when the human mind can make time stand still, if only for a second: that moment when we are 'hit' by true love. This may be the first time we meet someone, or it may be after years of having known them, but when it happens it is an experience that will stay with us our whole lives. And even if this love dies with time, the moment of its conception stays with us.

At that moment, we felt wholly content and sure that we would never want anyone else: we wanted to be with this person for the rest of our lives, and that was that. And yet time began to move again: we had managed to halt its progress – to make it stand still – only for a brief moment. From this moment on, we struggled against time. Time had the upper hand, and as time ticked away, never ceasing, the initial feelings of desire, lust and love all changed in their order of importance, and before long time took its toll, and the relationship deteriorated until it ended.

But time also has the opposite effect: it nurtures a need in people to stay together because they cannot stand to be on their own: it drives people to marry because they feel they *ought* to be married by a certain age: 'tick-tock the body clock' is always there, and they fear that if they do not do it now... tick-tock, tick-tock...well then they never will, and they cannot bear the thought of being consigned to the bachelor and spinster scrap heap until the end of time. Such marriages, attempting to press the pause button on life, are driven by an acute need not to be left behind, and often make for superficial and flimsy partnerships that end in no time at all.

Then there are others who marry out of genuine love, who believe that their love is strong enough to stand the test of time. It is as if such people believe that as long as they are married, their relationship will not be affected in the manner it would be were they not married: the institution will shield them against the effects of time, induce a kind of static bliss. And yet, in reality, their marriage is impotent. As time passes, they inevitably meet people who appear more interesting, more charming and more seductive than their spouse; and there finally comes a time when their libido usurps their logic and they yield to temptation, yearning to be inquisitive and adventurous once more.

Time is the breeder of complacency; complacency is the enemy of marriage. Temptation is rife; time and temptation will always take their toll... this much is certain. But, hey, give it time, and you'll be just fine.

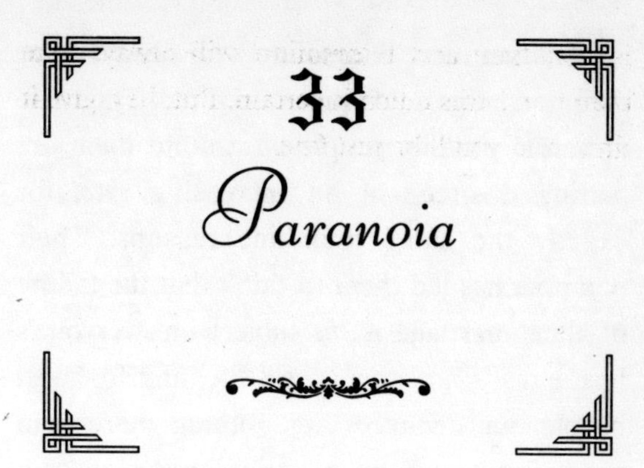

33 Paranoia

So once time has taken its toll and has driven our married couple apart, they now feel complete failures, and rightly so. They have failed, and must now face the world (and his ex-wife) as 'divorcees'. In fact, wherever our divorcees now go, they are looked upon as sad souls, pitied and condescended (to their face and behind their back) in equal measure. Ouch! That hurts, to be the centre of attention for such a painful and embarrassing reason. God, they even come to resent those who are kind, rather than cruel, to them: there is only so much melancholy they can take! And in light of all this, they are riddled with paranoia, sure that everyone sees them as complete failures.

And yet there is absolutely no need for our divorcees to be so damn self-centred. Their fate is hardly unique: people all around them are getting divorced at an increasing rate, for exactly the same mundane reasons. Their paranoia has led them to think that the failure of their marriage is *the* subject on everyone's lips, but it's not: this is real life, and for most people our divorcees are nothing more than a passing comment, a sympathetic sigh or a future conquest.

So divorcees…take heart! There is no need to be so far up your own arse. Life moves on, and so should you. You used to be depressed, lonely, miserable, aimless and married. You were stuck in a dead-ender; and just think, before that you were trying to find a dead-ender. Not any more, you now know where marriage will take you – through the wringer. And you won't be doing that again. Will you?!

34 Never Again

Now, all our divorcees need do is remain faithful to their prevailing post-marital instinct, which cries out, 'Never again, never again!' They must keep this gut feeling in mind; they must keep sight of it; they must vow to honour it until they die; they must remember that the *reality* of marriage is D.I.V.O.R.C.E.

If they remember these simple things, they will be happy.

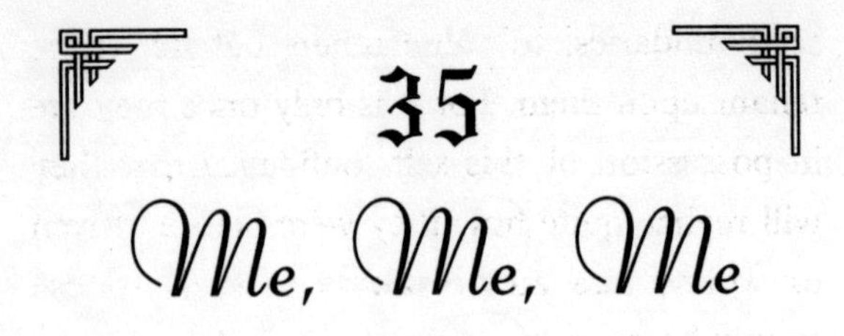

35 Me, Me, Me

Get selfish. Think of Number One. This is the only way for our divorcees to overcome their paranoia and to keep their vow never to marry again; it is now time to consider themselves rather than their damn spouses. They will fast learn that their previous existence – always wanting the best for their spouse and for the longevity of their (now defunct) marriage, rather than for themselves – was nothing more than a transparent cover for their ever-present and unattractive weakness, their neediness.

And let me stress that I am not advocating a kind of grotesque self-indulgence here. No, I am simply encouraging our divorcees to really know themselves; to appreciate themselves; to set boundaries; to value others but not to be reliant upon them. For it is only once they are in possession of this self-confidence that they will realize quite how they were before: driven to worry, fuss and obsess over their spouse simply because they thought they should, they knew of no other way, or they were just too pathetic to stand up for themselves.

Being needy is a truly unattractive quality, it drives people away; being strong and independent, now that's attractive.

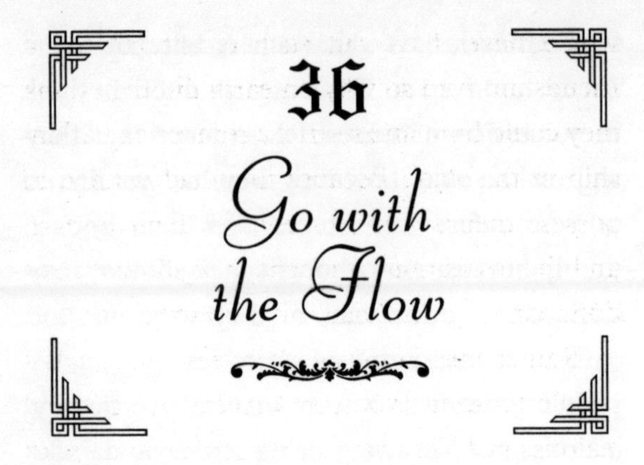

And so our divorcees suddenly become more aware of change. In fact, it now seems to them that everything around them is in a state of perpetual flux, this fills them with excitement, and they yearn to be a part of this diversity, to experience first hand the new people that enter their lives; the new places they encounter; the new situations they find themselves in. When they were married, they had had to resist change and temptation, but not now.

Indeed, it suddenly becomes clear to them quite how absurd the constriction of marriage is: they had never made a promise to any of their friends that the friendship would be exclusive, eternal and bound by law. Absolutely not. They would never have put such constraints on a friendship! And so why on earth did they think they could limit and restrict a romantic relationship in this way? Because they had wanted to possess their spouse, to control them forever, and the institution of marriage legitimized this dominant urge, fulfilled this emotional need.

Rather than resisting change, which makes people tense, nervous, possessive, uptight and jealous (just like marriage), it is time to go with the flow. Marriage as an institution is doomed, for the simple reason that it goes against the flow. It goes against change, against true, accepting, unconditional love. Marriage is, quite simply, unnatural.

Go with the flow of your life, and you might just find unconditional love.

37 The Speed of Life

Life is fast: it never ceases. Before we know it, we have finished school, we are out of university, we have found a job, we have married, and we are settling into our new home with our wife and kids. It has all happened so fast, and we have given it little serious thought. We have simply followed blindly and done what everyone else has done – education, job, house, spouse, children…blah, blah, blah, the generic and boring 'stepping stones' that must be followed to be a 'success' – and we have never really considered whether we want something different from life.

Now, though I must concede that there are a *few* happy marriages out there, these tend to be very old ones, formed when life was rather different, when it was more concerned with the community than the individual, with sustenance rather than consumption, when the roles of men and women were defined (unfairly, I grant you, but defined and understood all the same), a time when people walked to the shop; shoes were designed to last a decade not ten weeks; a suit aged gracefully with its owner; travel to another continent was an adventure and the post took a week to go across the country (oh, it still does); if you went bankrupt, you couldn't start up a new company with a different name the very next week, no – you were responsible for your actions, and you stuck by your decisions, good or bad.

Yet today, life is frantic and unstable. If we have to wait more than thirty seconds for our internet connection, we are irritable. Our food is fast and processed. We leave our children with childminders because we do not have time to look after them ourselves. We are unable to stop shopping, sure that our next purchase will bring us the bliss we crave. We talk on the phone at the same time as we speed down the motorway, drinking coffee from a disposable cup, listening to the radio, getting directions from our GPS. We do ten times the amount of things in a single day that our grandparents did in a week.

And yet, in spite of all this, we are surprised that we cannot sustain a relationship. No wonder we have such a high chance of being divorced in two years – that feels like a lifetime!

38

Celebration

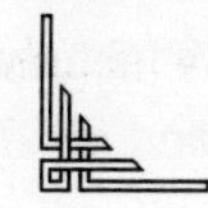

In this age of 'marital meltdown', where we seem unable to maintain our interest in anyone or anything for very long, I would like to give us all something to celebrate: the single life.

And when I speak of this, I am not imagining a world where there are only single people with no commitment or love for one another. No, I am advocating a world where two people love and enjoy one another 'for as long as they both shall *want*'...this could be for a day, a week, a month, a year or beyond.

It would be good to live in a world where we accept the *reality* of relationships and we embrace this reality as an opportunity to learn and grow, where we can love unconditionally without the fear of what might happen next.

At present when we meet someone for the first time, it is as if we are in an interview for some kind of lifelong job; there is enormous expectation attached right from the outset: immediately trying to ascertain whether there is any marital suitability. Why can't we simply enjoy meeting this person in the here and now? Why can't we just *be* with them? If the process was more for the enjoyment than for the outcome, the outcome would be far more enjoyable, and might actually lead to a mature, lasting and credible relationship, rather than an immature, fairytale-fuelled and vacuous attempt at 'true love'.

And so, instead of looking at the single life as a hole we have to climb out of, I would like to propose (I thought this was the most appropriate word) that we look at the single life as a time when we learn about ourselves and the people we are around. Rather than using this time to judge everyone for the prospects they might offer in the future, why not look at them as someone to enjoy right now – you never know where 'right now' might lead.

We currently live in a world of illusions. We enjoy our freedom, but every day is a day closer to having it taken away from us. Men are castrated by the expectations of marriage and family (that many of them do not want). And women are terrorized by the validation of a wedding, a husband and offspring (despite being unsure of these obligations at best, and terrified of them at worst). And, in the end, these fears usually amalgamate into an incredibly painful divorce that leads to a life of immense insecurity (which was the one thing they were both trying to avoid in the first place).

All of us are hurried and herded out of 'singledom' and enjoyment, by marriage, boredom, responsibility and dependence. Our fear of being alone controls (and consequently ruins) our lives; our desperation to procreate destroys our children; and our inability to stand up against our parents' wishes and the pressures of society terminates our independence.

We are a confusion by nature, let us not be a confusion by nurture. I urge you to celebrate the single life; to relish freedom; to enjoy the unknown.

39 Thoughts on Love

Love is a subjective experience, which resists definition. However, I shall nonetheless offer a very few thoughts on this inordinately complex notion. Firstly, it is always a privilege, even when it culminates in pain. Secondly, it differs every time we experience it. Thirdly, we should always strive to learn from it. Fourthly, no single love is final. Fifthly, its loss does not constitute its failure. And finally, to feel it is a good thing.

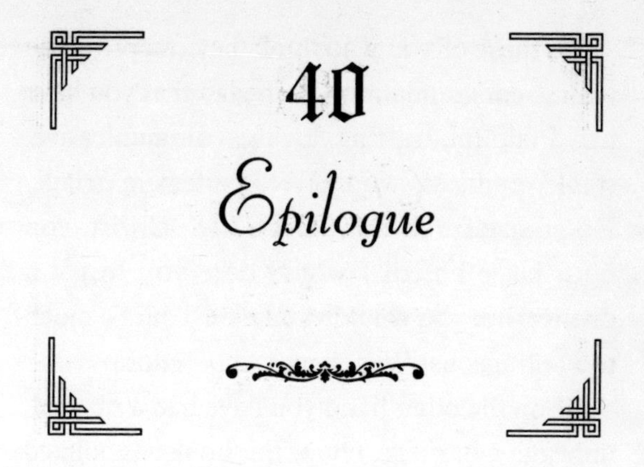

40 Epilogue

I would like to thank you for reading this book, assuming you have actually read the whole thing and have not simply turned to the final page.

I am aware that I have probably incensed some of you, and of this I am glad. In fact, if I have not enraged you in some way, then I have surely failed in my task. And whether you feel my opinions are right or wrong makes no difference, because you cannot argue with the fact that they are true – marriage is ultimately flawed, the statistics prove it, and if you do decide to marry, you will prove it too. You see, I wrote this book not only to comfort the disturbed, but more importantly to disturb the comfortable – to amuse, but also to challenge.

To those of you who think they can prove me wrong, congratulations. I am glad that you have had a faithful, trusting, loving, communicative, stable, painless, worry-free, perfect marriage. Do yourself a favour, 'Get a life'; Christ, you must be *so* bored! I would dare you to get a divorce, but you wouldn't take on a dare – much too outrageous! Well, here's to boredom.

If on the other hand you have had a normal, unhealthy marriage, I hope this book has pointed out some home truths, and I challenge you to either end the sham right now or at least be more aware of the gross imperfections of the institution you have entered into, and make the most of it nevertheless.

For the ones who still remain unconvinced by the ideas and arguments against marriage that I have put forward here, and are still intent on getting married, well I applaud you for your stubborn conviction, your short-sightedness, your fantastically juvenile dreams.

And finally, to those of you who have read this book and have been positively affected by it, then please, stay single, stay happy, and do not marry. There is simply no need to.